# From Me to You

STORIES ABOUT LIFE, LOVE, FAMILY, FAITH,
AND HOW TO NEGOTIATE A BIGGER ALLOWANCE

## Norman Aladjem

Post Hill
PRESS

A POST HILL PRESS BOOK
ISBN: 978-1-68261-809-7
ISBN (eBook): 978-1-68261-810-3

From Me to You:
Stories about Life, Love, Family, Faith, and How
to Negotiate a Bigger Allowance

Cover art by Cody Corcoran

Post Hill Press
New York • Nashville
posthillpress.com

Published in the United States of America

# Contents

For my sister, Vivien, who always told me I had a gift for writing,
and for my eleventh-grade English teacher, who always told me I didn't

BLESSED BEYOND MEASURE

# One: Why I'm Writing to You

Dear Mackenzie,

You were born exactly one month after my forty-fifth birthday. By then I was already blessed with two wonderful stepdaughters, Heather and Jamie. I hope I've had some hand in shaping Heather and Jamie into the amazing young women they've both become, but since they entered my life in their teens, I had neither the opportunity nor the responsibility to guide them through their early years.

Being an older dad has its pros and cons. On the one hand, I have come to believe that I can savor your childhood in a way that a younger dad cannot. It's not that a younger dad can't appreciate his young child. He most certainly can, and would. But being older, with my own career well established and with many life experiences under my belt, I feel better equipped to appreciate the miracle that is a young life. I don't take one bit of it for granted.

On the other hand, I can't afford to take anything for granted, because it's not certain I'll be around to watch you grow up. A young father who has a child at twenty-five or even thirty will still be in his forties when that child graduates from high school. Barring an accident of fate or of nature, he'll be there to guide his child into adulthood, to give him or her advice, and to provide comfort when his child skins a heart or skins a knee.

That's not necessarily so for an older dad. Since you were born, I find that I sometimes count my life expectancy in what I call "Mackenzie years." In other words, if I live to be, say, sixty-five, I'll see you through your high school years and into college. If I live to be eighty, I'll see you to thirty-five. And if I'm fortunate enough to live to be ninety, I'll see you to the age I was when you were born. Wow. But even with today's medical and biological advances, ninety, or eighty, or even sixty-five, is not promised in the way that forty-five or fifty is.

During the first few years of your life, I found myself telling your mom on many occasions how I hoped to savor the experience of your growing up. That there are so many things I want to say to you when you turn eighteen. And then when you get married. And then again when you have a child of your own. And so on. Don't get me wrong. I'm not obsessed with death or anything like that. On the contrary, my parents and grandparents have lived well into their seventies, eighties, and nineties, and I have every intention of doing the same.

And as I've said to your mom, if I were to die prematurely, who would teach you how to swing a bat or field a ground ball? Who would bore you with our favorite books and movies, or for that matter, who would remind you what your own favorites were when you were little? Or tell you who the fourteenth president of the United States was? (It was Franklin Pierce, by the way.)

Your mom has a wonderful sense of humor, by which I mean she laughs at my dumb jokes. She also indulges my lunacies with a serene patience. One day a few years ago, I was going on and on about what I wanted to tell you on your eighteenth birthday, and your mom, in part because she thought it was a good idea and in part to get me out of her hair, said to me, "Well, why don't you write it down?"

So I did. That kept me sane for a while. And then Jamie turned twenty-one, and I wrote her a letter for her twenty-first birthday. Don't worry, we gave her gifts too. And one day we were telling some friends about the day that you were born, and your mom thought that could make a great letter. And of course, I love telling the story of how your mom and I got together, so I thought I should write that one as well.

And then Heather, who at the time was living in Cleveland and loved to dance, tried out for the Cavaliers NBA dance squad. The night before the finals, I wrote Heather a letter from 2,500 miles away that I hoped would give her confidence and let her know that even though I wasn't there physically, I loved her and was rooting for her. I hope the letter helped Heather. I know it soothed my own aching heart, and served to lessen my sense of helplessness that I was not with her in a time of need.

So I started to think, why not keep writing these letters? Over time I plan to give you, Heather, and Jamie lots of advice, whether you want it or not. I plan to tell you lots of stories about your lives and ours. I plan to inspire you, to protect you, and to guide you. I plan to make you laugh, to console you when you are down, and to celebrate with you when you are happy. Yet maybe these letters can help if during some important moment, your mom and I are not around. Maybe many years from now you'll read the letters to your own children to pass on some family lore or, allowing for some personal vanity, to share some memories of your mom and the old man.

One final thing, which I hope you'll share with Heather and Jamie. These letters are yours, but the themes within them apply to you all. Once when you were about six, I was telling you how much I love you and your sisters. As befits a six-year-old, you asked me if I loved you best. In fact, I love the three of you in equal, boundless amounts; and everything in my heart, and all that I am, is for the three of you and your wonderful mom.

I hope you'll enjoy reading these letters, my sweet daughter, and that they will envelop you with all the love that I feel as I write them.

All my everlasting love,

Dad

THE STARLET SIGNING AUTOGRAPHS AFTER A SHOW

# Two: One Night in North Carolina

Dear Mackenzie,

At about 8:12 PM EST on Tuesday, November 18, 2008, in Raleigh, North Carolina, you said, "Momma, Momma, Mommy," and I started to cry. You said the words in a strong and booming voice. You were not at all in distress. And yet I couldn't stop the tears from flowing.

I don't know if I ever told you, my sweet daughter, but when he was a young man, your grandfather was a musical prodigy. He was an orchestra conductor and a composer of classical music. In his early teens, your grandfather went to Salzburg, Austria, along with several other young men from different parts of Europe, to audition for the noted conductor Herbert von Karajan.

Each of the candidates was asked to conduct a movement of a symphony with Karajan's orchestra while Karajan observed. One by one, your grandpa and the other young men (no women were allowed in those days) took their turn. As one of the candidates led Karajan's orchestra through a Mozart symphony (listen to Mozart's music sometime, it's magnificent), he worked up quite a sweat. According to your grandpa, when the young man finished, Karajan took the baton out of his hand and said dismissively, "This is Mozart. We don't sweat with Mozart." I love that story.

You might have inherited some of your creative genes from him. You certainly got creative genes from your sister Jamie. As you know, when Jamie was twelve she toured with the national Broadway tour of *Annie*, and whenever you saw anything related to *Annie*, you wanted to be in it, "just like Jamie."

When you were five, you auditioned for the role of Molly in a local children's production of *Annie*. At age four you had played a mouse in one of their productions of *Cinderella*, and the producer thought you were ready to "move up" to a speaking part. But at the audition you fell apart. It was very unlike you, as you'd been incredibly self-possessed and confident from the time you were born. Yet on that day, in that moment, when your turn came you froze. Even with the gentle coaxing of the producer and director, after a few tries you started to cry, said you didn't want to be in the play, and that was it.

On the ride home I imagined all sorts of horrible scenarios. I silently wondered if this would mark the beginning of an irreversible downward spiral in your life, your confidence ruined, your dreams shattered forever, drug and alcohol addiction just around the corner. Fortunately, your mom, being the uberparent she is, understood you had simply had a difficult moment, and consoled you as only a mother can. You asked if you could audition again next time, and with the resilience of a five-year-old, went on to other things. Or so it seemed.

In January 2008, your mom found out there was indeed another audition for *Annie*. But this time it wasn't for a pay-to-play kids' production. It was for a replacement cast for the national Broadway tour. At that audition Martin Charnin, the director and one of the creators of *Annie*, told your mom that they were not replacing the actress playing Molly, which was the only character you could play given your age, but that you had a lot of potential. He explained that if you took dance and voice lessons religiously for the next eight months, he would "be inclined to make you his next Molly" when the new tour went out in November. Both your mom and I were floored, and when your mom told you what Martin had said, you decided you wanted to pursue singing and dancing classes. And you did.

In June, the tour came to Southern California and we took you to see the show. As chance would have it, at intermission we saw Martin in the lobby and went to say hello. He was very nice, but it was clear that he had no recollection of you at all. I remember it dawning on me at the time that, like any good director who works with young people, he probably offered great encouragement to all the kids who exhibited the least bit of potential. Following the audition in January, Laura and I had started to wonder aloud how we would deal with six or more months of life on the road if in fact you got the next tour. After that encounter in the lobby, it felt obvious that no discussion was necessary, and we stopped talking about it altogether.

Then came September, and the auditions in New York for the new national tour. You were excited to go, and we wanted you to have a wonderful experience, but we were careful to manage your expectations. The audition dates coincided with the weekend of your seventh birthday, and we made a point of telling you the weekend in New York was a birthday present, with the audition just one part of the adventure. We also made plans for your friend Riley to come see you from Philadelphia, for Mom to take you to the fabulous American Girl store in the city, and who knows what else. Then off you and your mom went to the Big Apple.

Midday Saturday, your mom called me to say they were about to make the first round of cuts, and that you would be among them. I asked her how she could possibly know that, and she said you had come out during one of the breaks and told her they had not asked you to do some specific dance that the Molly character does. Your mom said she assumed that with so many kids auditioning, the creative team was simply being efficient with time when they determined someone was going to get cut anyway.

My heart sank. Obviously I wanted you to get the role if that was something you wanted. As important, like any parent, I was desperate for you not to feel the pain of rejection. I had secretly asked whatever higher power was out there that you'd at least make it through the first cut. You had worked very hard for this audition by any standard, let alone that of a six-year-old. I hoped you would be able to experience a little of that wonderful feeling of achievement and fulfillment that ideally should always accompany hard work and commitment but all too often doesn't. I hung up, tried to imagine what might be going through your tender mind, and thought about what I could say to you when we spoke that might provide you both comfort in the present and inspiration for the future.

I also tried not to look at the clock. About an hour later when the phone rang, I desperately didn't want to answer it. But when I did, your mom told me you had made the first cut. When I could breathe again, I congratulated you on your great work and then relaxed. Prayer answered. The phone rang again a couple of hours later, then once or twice more after that, and each time your mom was calling to say you had survived another cut. By day's end you were one of the finalists going back Sunday morning.

I had a sleepless night. I was certainly no longer relaxed, and I felt helpless to do anything except worry. Early Sunday morning your mom called and said it looked like you were one of two for the role of Molly. The final phone call came around noon. I will always remember your mom's words when I picked up the phone. "Hi, honey," she said lightly. "Mackenzie wants to tell you something."

Six weeks later, you and Mom got on a plane to Jacksonville, Florida, to start rehearsals, and three weeks after that I sat in a darkened theater in Raleigh, North Carolina, my heart pounding, your mother's hand in mine. At about 8:12 PM EST, the curtain went up on the 2008–2009 national Broadway tour of *Annie*. "Momma, Momma, Mommy," said Molly, the youngest orphan, and I began to cry.

All my everlasting love,

Dad

YOUR MOM, THE "IT GIRL"

# Three: How I Met Your Mother

Dear Mackenzie,

This is a story about the hand of God, what in the Jewish tradition we call *b'sheret.* This is the story of your mother and me.

Your mom was the most popular girl at Cleveland Heights High School. She was the "It" girl. She was the perky, friendly, beautiful, blonde, green-eyed cheerleader whom every girl wanted to be friends with and every boy wanted to date. I was no exception, and I was in love with her from afar. Unfortunately I was not the "it" anything, and your mom didn't know me.

One night at the local skating rink, I saw my big chance to ask her out. Your mom was there with some friends, probably watching her hockey-player boyfriend, and I went up to her and said, "Hi, Laura." "Hi," she answered sweetly. After an awkward silence during which I couldn't summon the courage to say anything further, she drifted away.

High school ended and your mom and I both went on with our respective lives. She went to Ohio State and then got married, became a mom, and moved to Pennsylvania. I went to law school in California, stayed, and went to work in the entertainment industry. That was it for your mom and me for many years.

Now, my sweet daughter, you may be wondering how this is a story about the hand of God. Aside from a fleeting moment at a skating rink, our lives could not have been more disconnected if we had tried. But listen to this.

Sometime in 1998, I had lunch with a Hollywood producer named Marc Sternberg (in Hollywood a lot of business is done over meals), and it turned out he was also from Cleveland. Marc told me about a successful talent manager named Heidi Rotbart who had gone to the same high school as your mom and me. Then she and I went to lunch (see what I mean about meals in Hollywood?), became friends, and I told her about my secret high school crush on Laura Givner.

Heidi knew your mom and told me Laura was married, had two children, and lived in Pennsylvania. That news gave me a twinge of regret, but to be fair, didn't rock me the way a story about ill-fated lovers could or should have. After all, our love affair had played out many years earlier, and solely in my own head. I attributed the regret I felt to things left unsaid or undone generally in my younger days, and didn't give it much more thought than that.

Then in early 1999, Heidi called me. "Guess what?" she teased. "Laura Givner is in town. Want to join us for dinner?" At the time, of course, I never imagined a future with your mom. I simply assumed my strong desire to see her was of the "what happened to the 'It' girl?" variety, not of the "she's my soul mate" variety. But the dinner never materialized, and I let it go.

Several months later, your mom, who by now was back in Pennsylvania, sent me an email. She said that she'd gotten my email address from Heidi, and that she had been married but now was divorced. She wrote a bit about Heather and Jamie, and asked me how I'd been for the past twenty years. What she didn't say, but which was actually the case, was that she had no idea who I was.

I was by then in my early forties, successful, and confident about my place in the world. Yet if your mom had said she didn't remember me, I might have reverted to my high school insecurities and that would have been the end of us. But she didn't, and so I didn't. Thus the story can continue.

Naturally every story about fate and love includes the part where the gods toy with the lovers, and this one is no exception. Since your mom didn't remember me, she looked up my picture in our high school yearbook. Because the gods have a great sense of humor, that year my picture had been transposed with that of another student. And although I don't look like Brad Pitt, I do look like Brad compared to the guy whose picture she saw when she looked me up. He was a goofy-looking kid: funny ears; big, frizzy hair; not at all grown into himself. Who knows? Maybe he grew up to look like Brad Pitt. I hope so.

Now in those days I traveled to New York with some frequency, and after that email I would always suggest to your mom that she drive to the city and meet me for dinner. She would always decline (re-read the preceding paragraph to see why). One day I finally said, "I think I'll take the train to Philadelphia and come see you. What's your home address?" That got your mother to New York.

On December 18, 1999, your mom, along with her two friends Sally Comisarow and Sue Furfari, drove to Manhattan from Bucks County, Pennsylvania. I had no idea she was bringing bodyguards, and I had made us a reservation at a restaurant called Joe Allen's. Your mom had told me she loved Broadway shows, and Joe Allen's was a favorite eatery for the Broadway crowd. Maybe I thought that would impress her. And they served a mean banana cream pie to boot.

Waiting for Laura in the lobby of my hotel, I wasn't particularly nervous. That is, until I saw her. Wow! My heart skipped a beat, and then skipped another one. Your mom didn't recognize me at all, even when I said hello. I wasn't the guy in the picture, but I wasn't anyone else she knew either.

Unbeknownst to me, Sally and Sue were standing about twenty yards away checking me out, but they didn't reveal themselves. Laura told me about them only once we were at Joe Allen's, and she said we'd meet up with them after dinner at the Olive Garden restaurant in Midtown, where they were waiting for us.

As I said, it was December, and cold, and I was wearing the long, gray overcoat I used to wear when I went back east during winter. We had walked into the Olive Garden to find Sally and Sue, and your mom started to walk upstairs. I'd never been to that restaurant and didn't know there was an upstairs. As I started to walk past the stairs, your mom took hold of me by my coat. There was nothing particular in it. A casual observer could have described the movement as simply one person guiding another by their overcoat. But to me it came across as intensely intimate, sensual, and loving. I don't know why. Yet the moment remains a vivid memory of the instant I knew I wanted to be with your mom forever, and this time for real.

We all walked to see the Christmas tree at Rockefeller Plaza like two high school kids and their chaperones. I owe Sue and Sally a lot, and I won't forget what they did for your mom and me. I found out much later they had pushed Laura to come to New York to meet me, finally sealing the deal by agreeing to go with her, and they subsequently cheered us on in the early days when your mom was skeptical about getting into a long-distance relationship.

A couple of days later your mom drove back into the city, alone this time, and we went to see *Putting It Together*, the Stephen Sondheim musical that was starring Carol Burnett and our agency's client Ruthie Henshall. Afterward we stood in the freezing cold waiting for her car, which was parked in one of those outdoor vertical parking lots on Eighth Avenue that are unique to New York. Finally I turned to kiss her and suddenly I was back in high school, the "It" girl in my arms at long last. I remember thinking as we kissed that if I had to die right then, at least I had experienced that moment.

Your mom and I wish you many such moments, Mackenzie. They're not all romantic ones, of course. I had that magical feeling when you were born. I had that feeling one night a few years ago when Heather called, elated that she had made the cheer squad for the San Diego Shockwave. I had that feeling watching your aunt Viv walk down the aisle with her husband. I had that feeling teaching Jamie to drive, even as she was banging up my very expensive car. Most important, I still have that feeling every time I look at your mom and know that finally, really, we are together.

All my everlasting love,

Dad

SECOND CLASS
AIR MAIL

WHO'S THAT BABY?

# Four: On the Day That You Were Born

Dear Mackenzie,

September 11, 2001 was a dark day. The terrible events in New York, Washington, D.C., and Pennsylvania shocked and saddened your mom and me, and most of the world. It was an abject lesson on the horrible things people can do. Yet for your mom and me, 9/11 also was and remains one of the happiest days of our lives.

Since you have two older sisters, you know that your mom was no novice when it came to being pregnant. She's also very considerate and never wants to inconvenience people. Both facts are relevant to this story.

Because the physical act of childbirth can be very painful for the mother, a birthing technique was developed in the 1940s by a French obstetrician named Fernand Lamaze to help moms cope with the pain. The Lamaze method focuses on proper breathing, soothing massages (your mom's personal favorite), and so on.

At our Lamaze class, your mom told me she wanted to experience your birth the same way she had experienced Heather's and Jamie's births, naturally and without the help of pain medication. I didn't want your mom to suffer any more pain than necessary, but I took comfort in the fact that she knew what she was doing.

Big-city life being what it is, Mom's obstetrician, Stephen Rabin, was called as an expert witness at a trial in Palm Springs. He was scheduled to testify on September 12, which was right around your mom's due date. Your mom and I wanted Dr. Rabin to deliver you, so we agreed that sometime on the afternoon of September 11, Dr. Rabin would induce labor (don't ask me how) and deliver you that evening before leaving town. I would come home at lunch and off we'd go. Man plans and God laughs, as the saying goes.

At about 2:00 AM on the morning of the 11th, I woke up to your mom having severe Braxton Hicks contractions. Braxton Hicks is like false labor. For lack of a better explanation, it's the body rehearsing how it will get the baby out. I immediately went into full battle mode, asking your mom how far apart her contractions were, how long each was lasting, and whatever else I'd been taught to ask. I also insisted we call Dr. Rabin immediately.

Your mom was having none of it and didn't want to bother Dr. Rabin in the middle of the night. She chuckled at my naiveté and gently suggested I go back to sleep. At 2:45 AM I woke up again to find your mom still wrestling with her Braxton Hicks contractions. Again I urged calling the doctor, and again she demurred. "Honey," she said, "there's no reason to wake him. I'm fine." Then she had another contraction, which seemed to last forever, after which she said that with this pregnancy she might take drugs after all.

That was it for me. If your mom of all people was talking about taking drugs, she was in full-blown labor whether she knew it or not. Over her objection, I woke Dr. Rabin and filled him in. He told me to get your mom to the hospital "as soon as humanly possible" and that he would meet us there.

Yikes. I woke Jamie (we had driven Heather to San Diego to start college a week or so earlier), rushed everyone into the car, and started driving to the hospital like a madman. By the way, your mom would probably say I always drive like a madman and her labor only gave me an excuse in case the police stopped us. She's wrong, of course. I'm an excellent driver. Sometimes I'm just inattentive. Well, that's my story and I'm sticking with it.

In any event, we arrived at the Cedars-Sinai emergency room at 3:45 AM. An obstetrics nurse examined your mom, pronounced that she was fully effaced and ten millimeters dilated (wide open and ready to go, for those of us who are not doctors), and sent us immediately to a delivery room. She said the baby—you—was about to come and it was too late for an epidural. Then Dr. Rabin arrived and chastised me (!!!) for waiting so long to call him.

Dr. Rabin got Mom settled and hooked her up to a machine designed to monitor the baby's heartbeat. He was a bit concerned that you weren't "coming down the chute" quickly enough given the full dilation, so he decided to manually "break Mom's water" (no, I don't know what that means either). Dr. Rabin also instructed me to watch the fetal monitor and let him know if it went under 100 heartbeats per minute. Then he left the room, probably to ingest some caffeine.

As you know, Mackenzie, your grandpa is an obstetrician, and a really good one. During your mom's pregnancy, I had asked him a million questions and he always took the time to calm my nerves. Sometime after you were born, your grandpa told me with great amusement that an obstetrician will often ask the dad to keep an eye on the fetal heart monitor if the dad seems overly nervous. The assignment gives a nervous dad something specific to do while basically keeping him out of harm's way. I also tried to do all the things I had learned in Lamaze class. In hindsight I was probably a great nuisance, but your mom was kind enough not to call me on it.

Then suddenly it happened. Without warning, the fetal monitor fell from 120 to 110 to 100, and then to 60 in a matter of a few seconds. I couldn't believe my eyes. Trying not to sound as alarmed as I felt, I called the nurse and asked her to look at the monitor. The nurse's reaction to the precipitous drop in your heart rate confirmed to me what I couldn't bear to think. Both you and Mom were in trouble.

Dr. Rabin exploded into the room, which suddenly resembled a M\*A\*S\*H\* unit. He started barking orders, and nurses were running around. Out of nowhere two other doctors, who I subsequently learned were neonatal crisis specialists, stood at the door like a SWAT team, game faces on and in full surgical gear. Dr. Rabin didn't acknowledge them, but I suspect he was the one who had gotten them there.

Dr. Rabin locked eyes with your mom. "Laura," he said, calm yet in charge. "Look at me. The cord is wrapped around the baby's neck. That's why the heart rate keeps dropping. We have to get the baby out *now! Push! Push! Push!*"

My heart was stuck in my throat. "Dear Lord," I silently prayed with fervor I didn't know I possessed. "Please don't take my wife and daughter from me." Dr. Rabin continued to coach. Your mom continued to push. I continued to pray.

When I was in college, my sweet daughter, sometimes I would donate blood at the Red Cross to make a little cash. One day while giving blood I panicked and started to hyperventilate. The doctor had me breathe into a paper bag, and within seconds my breathing stabilized. I was unhooked and given some orange juice. A few minutes later the doctor came over to see how I was doing, and I told him I was fine. "That's why I make the big bucks," he chuckled. "For giving me a paper bag?" I smiled. "For knowing to have you breathe into it," he said, smiling back.

And so it was with Dr. Rabin. Somehow, between his focus with Mom and some weird conelike gizmo he used, at 4:36 AM PST on the morning of September 11, 2001, you hurtled into this world. Dr. Rabin confirmed that everything was normal, and I took my first breath in forever. Once Dr. Rabin did his so-called Apgar evaluation (you scored a nine, if you want to know), he gave the two SWAT doctors the slightest of nods, and they were gone. Just another day at the office.

The relief, exultation, and unbridled love we felt as we held you in our arms are difficult to put into words even now. I took dozens of pictures, only to find out later that in the craziness of the moment I had forgotten to put film in the camera! (This was before digital photos.) Yet nothing could dampen our bliss.

And then about an hour later, the planes hit the towers and the world turned upside down. But even in the context of that tragedy, you reminded us on that day, as you do every day, that no matter how dark things get there is always light. You also reminded us that sometimes you have to fight for that light, and pray for it, and push for it as if your very life depended on it. You, along with Heather and Jamie, are our eternal light.

All my everlasting love,

Dad

SPECIAL DELIVERY

# Five: The Birds and the Bees

Dear Mackenzie,

Everything you need to know about the birds and the bees can be found in Alfred Hitchcock's 1963 film *The Birds* and the 2007 animated comedy *Bee Movie*, which stars the voice of Jerry Seinfeld. Strike that.

Dear Mackenzie,

Everything you need to know about the birds and the bees can be found in the 1972 film *Last Tango in Paris* starring Marlon Brando and the 1971 film *Carnal Knowledge* starring Jack Nicholson. *Really* strike that.

Dear Mackenzie,

Not I but your mother, since she is very eloquent on these types of issues, will teach you everything you need to know about the birds and the bees. Well, probably true but a bit of a cop out. Try again.

Dear Mackenzie,

Hmmm. This is awkward.

Dear Mackenzie,

As you'll probably already know by the time you read this, "the birds and the bees" is an idiomatic expression that refers to courtship and sex. It's a difficult topic for parents to discuss with their children and for children to discuss with their parents. It's an especially difficult topic for fathers to discuss with their daughters. To make things even more complicated, birds and bees don't have sex in any way similar to humans from a biological perspective, though I've detected certain sociological similarities.

Most bird species are monogamous in one form or other, and some birds mate for life. This trait alone sets them apart from a majority of humans, who say they are monogamous but rarely are, and certainly not while they are young, which is when human parents most want them to be. Some birds mate on the ground, while others mate in trees. Well, there's that similarity. In addition to the ground and trees, humans have also been known to mate on top of pool tables, in the back seats of cars, on moving roller coasters, and generally anywhere that the body parts can be positioned in the right way. By the way, bees almost always mate in the air—a sort of bee "mile-high club" that many humans try to emulate. More on bees in a minute.

Both birds and humans engage in so-called courtship displays. In the human species, the female uses makeup and other items (let's call them plumage) to show the male how attractive and desirable she is. Birds are the opposite. In the bird kingdom, it's the male who will usually preen or make sounds (let's call that plumage also) to show the female how attractive and desirable he is to her. A perfect example is the peacock, and I don't think the name is an accident.

The bird courtship ritual I like the best is that of the hummingbird. To show its desirability, the male hummingbird flies up and then dive-bombs toward the female at full speed, diverting his course only inches from her head. A college classmate of mine once tried something similar with a pretty co-ed to express his desirability. Unfortunately, he had gone through a full bottle of Jägermeister and was several sheets to the wind by the time he did it. For obvious reasons, his hand-eye coordination was a little off, and they both wound up in a hospital emergency room, he with a concussion and she with numerous stitches above her left eye. Unlike the hummingbird, my friend's particular courtship ritual ended up not in a successful mating encounter but in a court of law.

Most birds become more sexually active in the spring when the amount of sunlight they receive sends signals to their brains that it is time to reproduce. In the human species, this is more gender-specific. Most females indeed seem to send out courtship and mating signals in the spring, when the weather gets warm and the sun and heat suggest it may be an opportune time to mate. Males are somewhat different. In humans, the male of the species becomes more sexually active when…well, when he can. The only thing a male needs is opportunity. It's usually that simple.

Which brings us to bees. It has been written in scientific journals that the sole purpose of the life of the male bee is to have sex. Coincidentally, that is also the sole purpose in life for the young male human. Now, that's nice if you're a male, unless you're a male human whose daughters are pursued by young males. As the father of three daughters myself, I admit that the fate of the male honey bee sometimes sounds appropriate to me. When the male honey bee inserts his sexual organ into the female, it becomes lodged and remains in the female, and since the male cannot survive without his sexual organ, he dies shortly thereafter. I think about handing out this scientific literature to the young men who currently court Heather and Jamie and explaining to them that I envision a similar fate for them. Mackenzie, I can't even imagine what thoughts will cross my mind by the time boys come calling for you in a few years.

Though not a bird or a bee, the sexually toughest cookie, by far, is the female praying mantis, and as the father of three girls, the fate of the male praying mantis also intrigues me. The female praying mantis has the peculiar cannibalistic habit of biting off the head of her partner while they are mating. One shot and crunch, you're history. If you're a male praying mantis, you'd better be committed, because you're not going to get a second encounter. In my mind's eye, the same theory could apply to the young men who have the wrong thoughts about my daughters.

Truth be told, my sweet daughter, biology is only the half of it. That is what it is, and we'll try to explain it all to you as best we can. As your dad, I worry more about the emotional toll that the life lessons of the birds and bees can take on a young person. In spite of your mother's and my best efforts, your real teacher will be life itself and the wisdom that can only come from experience. That said, I do have one or two pieces of advice to offer.

But first, time out for an important medical announcement: *always use a condom when you're having sex.*

Once you're in a long-term committed relationship, or married, or trying to conceive children of your own, you may decide not to use condoms. But while you're single and experimenting, this is an absolute must. Not just as a form of contraception, which you should always use until you make the decision to have children, but for reasons of life and death. AIDS is no joke, and can literally kill you. AIDS is not a gay disease. It's not a poor person's disease. It's not a disease borne of poor hygiene, or related to any particular religion, race, or gender. It doesn't discriminate. It's an equal opportunity killer, plain and simple. With any luck, the medical community will find a cure one of these days, or may even figure out how to prevent HIV and AIDS.

Until then, time out for an important medical announcement: a*lways use a condom when you're having sex.*

Mackenzie, always be proud of your body and enjoy it to the fullest. The human body is the most amazing instrument in so many ways and can bring great pleasure and joy to both you and your partner. Don't let anyone convince you that sex is bad. Don't let anyone convince you that sex is not for the woman's enjoyment or pleasure. Don't let anyone convince you that sex is shameful, or should be hidden from light, or is in any way abnormal, no matter what crazy fantasies titillate you.

(I can't believe I'm writing this to you…awkward.)

So yes, go crazy. Experiment to your heart's content. Have fun. Think outside the box. Be wild in a safe way. Never stop. And whatever you do, Mackenzie, never, never, and I do mean never, share any of that with me!!!  Did I mention to never share that stuff with me? I don't even know how much of that you should share with your mother, but me? *Nada. Niente.* Nothing. Never.

You should also know that the life lessons learned from the birds and the bees have twin engines of hope and despair, of euphoria and desperation, of pleasure and pain (and I don't mean S&M). It's not easy for any person, let alone a young person, to completely disconnect his or her hormones from their hearts and from their minds. When one partner is more emotionally attached than the other, and even if both partners are equally attached emotionally, the birds and the bees can cause heartache and tears. There is no getting around it.

For all the delicious excitement you will experience, from time to time you will also experience a broken heart accompanied by a seemingly tragic sense of despair. As much as your mom and I would give anything to shield you from the downside of the birds-and-the-bees phenomenon, we simply can't. Everyone needs to go through it themselves. We can only love and support you unconditionally when you are sad, lend you our shoulders and our ears when you need them, and carry you forward as and when we are able. In those difficult moments we will tell you, though it will be hard for you to believe at that time, that this too shall pass.

From what I know of you so far, Mackenzie, I suspect you'll attack this topic with the same passion and gusto that you've shown for everything else that has come your way in life. That thrills me and scares the living daylights out of me all at once. Your mom and I, and your older sisters, will be there for you when you need us. But please. Be gentle with us. I don't know if your education in the birds and bees will be overly hard on you, but I can only imagine its toll on us.

All my everlasting love and with a shotgun at the ready,

Dad

# Six: The Perils of Advice

Dear Mackenzie,

Periodically I get the opportunity to speak at colleges and universities around the country. As you may know, I love public speaking. I'm a big hambone for starters, so I love the attention and the applause. I also get great personal fulfillment from teaching and inspiring young minds.

Given what I do for a living, whenever I lecture I'm asked lots of questions about show business. Students ask me how to get an agent. They ask me how to get their films produced. They ask me how to become successful actors, writers, and directors. Those are all important questions, and I answer them as best I can. But as I look at life from my vantage point today, what I wish someone had told me when I was in school is something altogether different.

Our family immigrated to the United States when I was eight years old. I started the third grade in a new country, not knowing a single word of English and without a single friend. I was an outsider. I was disoriented. I wanted desperately to assimilate.

Throughout my youth, the people positioned to guide my thinking told me all the things I couldn't do. Things I couldn't do because I was an immigrant, or because of my height (or lack of it), or because our family was not rich. No doubt they were trying to help and protect me, but the advice I got from these so-called mentors was wrong. What I want to pass on to you is what I wish they had told me instead.

Don't let fear paralyze you. There is nothing innately wrong with fear. It may save your life one day, figuratively or even literally. Fear is a survival mechanism hardwired into our reptilian brain. Let fear work for you when necessary, but don't let it overtake you.

Too many people don't follow their dreams and live unfulfilled lives because they are afraid to fail. They are afraid to be rejected. They are afraid to look foolish.

You be the opposite. Be afraid not to try. Be afraid not to risk. Be afraid not to live your life as fully as you deserve. Take at least one chance every day on behalf of your heart. Take at least one chance every day in your career. Take at least one chance every day in everything that gives your life meaning. You'll win a few and lose a few. You'll laugh more than you can imagine and cry more than you think you can bear. But you'll never regret reaching for the stars. Les Brown, the well-known motivational speaker, likes to say that when most people die, their epitaph could easily read, "Dead but not used up." Don't just exist, my sweet daughter. Live!

Have a love of learning. I don't necessarily mean academics, although the two often go hand in hand. But I hope as you continue to develop, you'll love to read. I hope you'll have a native curiosity about biology, or literature, or comparative religion, or lacrosse and its lore, or fashion, or astronomy, or any of the things that make life and humanity so miraculous. I was never a particularly great student, but somewhere along the way I fell in love with reading. I found that books helped me escape to faraway places. I found that they gave shape to my innermost feelings and gave voice to my opinions and beliefs. Books have given me an appreciation of the beauty of language that has enriched my life immensely. May you have that same glorious experience.

And finally, believe in yourself. Others will perceive you as you perceive yourself, and to quote Eleanor Roosevelt, no one can make you feel inferior without your consent. My paternal grandfather (your great-grandfather) was a fascinating person. You would have loved him, and he would have adored you. He was intelligent, passionate, caring, and courageous. When I was in college, he and I spent many hours at his dining room table discussing everything under the sun. While my grandmother fed us until we were ready to burst, we'd talk politics, love (he and his wife were married for more than sixty years), religion, and anything else that crossed our minds.

By then he was already in his mid-seventies. In the mid-1940s, when my grandfather was about fifty, he moved his entire family from Europe to South America to start a new life in Uruguay. He did not speak one word of Spanish at the time. Imagine that! Imagine having to start all over at fifty in a country where you don't even speak the language. Yet your great-grandfather did just that. He learned Spanish, and then he rose to a high level at the company where he worked in Montevideo. I suspect running from the Nazis was a pretty good motivator too.

At age seventy, he and my grandma Lilly decided they wanted to be closer to us, so they picked up and moved continents again. My grandfather spoke no English, but he got a job as a bookkeeper in Cleveland, because he didn't want my grandmother and himself to be dependent on my parents. At seventy! I once asked him how he managed to do all that in his life. "I believed in myself," he told me, "and I knew if I believed in myself, then others would too."

Mackenzie, you have been blessed with God-given gifts. As I write this letter, you seem to have a passion and a talent for the arts. Maybe those will remain lifelong pursuits. But who knows? You're ten. Maybe as you get older, you'll discover that you have a mind for science. Maybe as you get older, you'll love carpentry instead, or archaeology, or planting flowers. Maybe you'll understand the value of baseball cards and make a life out of that. Maybe in the future when you look under the hood of a car, you'll see art.

Use these gifts however they unfurl. Savor them without apology. Go forth and fulfill your destiny. And may all your impossible dreams come true.

All my everlasting love,

Dad

# Seven: Life's Crucibles

Dear Mackenzie,

We're all tested in life now and again. About four years ago, when Heather tried out for the Cleveland Cavaliers dance squad, she went through quite a crucible. Here is the letter I wrote to her on June 28, 2008, on the eve of the finals. I'm grateful that Heather is letting me share it with you. Enjoy, my sweet daughter, and maybe it will help you one day.

　　All my everlasting love,

　　Dad

*Dear Heather,*

*First of all, congratulations on making it to the finals. I knew you would be there! We're all very proud of you. I can only imagine how physically and mentally drained you must be, and I suspect tomorrow will be more of the same. There are a few things I hope you can keep in mind.*

*　　First and most importantly, I can promise you that without exception every other person who made it to the finals is feeling exactly the same as you. The same exhaustion. The same anxiety. The same fear that everyone else is more confident, better rested, and more prepared than they are. That may be hard to believe in this moment, but it's true. As you can probably attest from what you yourself may be feeling, being outwardly poised does not make your inner feelings any less excruciating.*

*I suspect that a number of the other young women who will be competing against you in the finals tomorrow are current or former Cavs cheerleaders, or have been on local teams like the one you were on in San Diego, or appear to be friends with each other. That might concern you and make you think they have a leg up on you. But they don't, and they are thinking exactly the opposite. To you it looks like they have great camaraderie. To them it's the reverse. They look at you as unburdened by their existing rivalries and petty internal fights.*

*You may be thinking that the judges look at them as the tried and true. They fear the judges look at them as old news and look at you as the fresh, hot new blood they're convinced the Cavs are looking for. You wonder if they have an advantage because they've been to local workshops. They wonder what workshops you've attended, and what moves you know that they do not.*

*Take it from someone who has competed his whole life and has studied the dynamics of competition. Everyone there, and I mean everyone, is worried that you (and everyone else) are about to take their spot.*

*Three thoughts about the exhaustion, fear, or anxiety you may experience tomorrow:*

- *10 hours or less from when you read this, it will be over. You can sustain anything for 10 hours. The adrenaline alone will get you there.*

- *A friend of mine was a very successful wrestler in college. If you've ever seen a collegiate wrestling match, it's seven minutes of brutal, unyielding isometric torture. I once asked my friend how he got through it. He told me that no matter how exhausted he was during a match, or how ready to give up, he always knew that his opponent was equally exhausted and that his opponent's psyche was as strained to the breaking point as his was. He said all he had to do was endure just a little bit longer than the other guy.*

- *I have no idea if this is true, but years ago when Sylvester Stallone was making one of the Rambo movies, I heard a great story. Supposedly during production in the desert, the temperature repeatedly got so brutally hot that Stallone kept passing out from heat exhaustion. Finally someone suggested to him that they should simply move the production inside to an air-conditioned sound stage.*

  *Stallone apparently responded that once filming was over, he would forget his exhaustion and fainting spells quickly enough. But that for the rest of his life he would remember his effort to make a great film. And so I say that to you as well. By tomorrow night, and certainly within a few days, you'll be fresh as a daisy again. What will stay with you forever is what you leave on the dance floor tomorrow.*

*One final thought, about staying in the moment. I once heard about a long jumper who had just won the gold medal in the Olympics and was being interviewed. He explained that in the year prior to the Olympics, every day he would put on the same old pair of sweats, go into the empty rickety gym near his house, and practice. Before each jump he would envision himself about to make his third and final jump with the gold medal on the line. He envisioned the fifty thousand screaming fans in the stadium and the fifty million people watching on television. And then he would jump. Over and over and over. He did it a thousand times.*

*Sure enough, at the Olympics he found himself in the very situation he had imagined and worked for every day. He stepped up for his third and final jump with Olympic gold on the line. Fifty thousand fans screamed and cheered. Fifty million people around the world held their breath as they watched his every move. The overriding magnificent obsession of his life hung in the balance.*

*The interviewer asked him what the moment had felt like, being in that overwhelming situation for real. The athlete answered that he didn't really remember. He said that when he got up for his final attempt at gold, he simply envisioned himself in his old pair* of sweats, in the same empty rickety gym where he had jumped a thousand times, and just went about the business of jump one thousand and one.

I guess what I'm saying is, stay in the moment tomorrow. Don't get overwhelmed by what might or might not happen. Just go out and do what you love to do. Remember that line about "dance as if no one is watching"? Do that. Don't play it safe. Don't worry about being embarrassed. Don't worry about failing. Don't leave it inside you.

You can do this, Heather.

It is in you.

You have the look.

You have the talent.

You have worked and prepared for this day.

You've earned it and you deserve it.

Take it. Feel it. Savor it.

Make it yours.

You won't regret it.

All my love and more. xoxo

Norm

JAMIE SERENADING US AT OUR WEDDING

# Eight: Our Wedding Day

Dear Mackenzie,

The other day I started to contemplate what I might say to you on your wedding day, and my mind wandered instead to the memories of your mom's and my own wedding.

Your mom had just moved to Los Angeles when she and I planned our big day. Since we didn't belong to a temple, we set about finding someone to marry us. As it turns out, Los Angeles has a number of itinerant rabbis who, as the saying goes, are available for weddings and bar mitzvahs. A couple we knew had recently used one such rabbi. They told us he was wonderful and that he was a very poetic speaker. So your mom and I went to see him.

The rabbi was very genial, but over the course of our meeting he asked very little beyond when and where we were getting married. After fifteen minutes or so he stood up and said he looked forward to seeing us at the event. Your mom and I were a little unsettled. Poetic speaker or not, we didn't want a generic ceremony. We asked the rabbi whether some personal information about us would be appropriate, and he suggested we email him what we wanted to include, assuring us he would "work it in."

As you might imagine, we started having second thoughts about using him. When we told our good friends Betty and John Power what had happened, they suggested we meet a young rabbi named Paul Kipnes. We were immediately taken with him. Rabbi Kipnes was completely engaged, and he told your mom that I was an amazing man and that she was fortunate to be marrying me. Okay, fine, I'm making that last part up.

Once we decided that Rabbi Kipnes would officiate at our wedding, we were left with the uncomfortable task of dismissing the first rabbi. Though we sensed that he wasn't particularly invested, he was still a man of God, and your mom made the executive decision that I should be the one to call him. Now in truth, I have dozens of difficult conversations every week in my work. Yet when it came to having one with a rabbi, I was terrified.

When I finally got up the courage, I was told that the rabbi was traveling, so I left a weak message that maybe he should call me. When I didn't hear back, I decided to take the easy way out. Rather than calling again, I wrote the rabbi an email telling him we were joining a temple and would be using their rabbi. That wasn't true of course, but what can I say? Welcome to the politics of fear.

On September 24, 2000, at 5:00 PM, your mom and I were to be married at a beautiful restaurant on Ventura Boulevard called the Bistro Gardens. Yet by 4:30 PM, Rabbi Kipnes was still nowhere to be found. As I greeted our guests, the clock moved inexorably toward the appointed hour. I became increasingly alarmed by Rabbi Kipnes' absence, and it must have shown on my face because people started telling me it was normal for the groom to be nervous on his wedding day. For the record, my sweet daughter, I wasn't one bit nervous about marrying your mom. On the contrary, I couldn't wait to do it. But where the hell was the rabbi?

At 4:55 PM, someone tapped me on the shoulder. I turned around to see…the first rabbi! He had a prayer book in his hand and a big smile on his face. "Ready to get married?" he asked.

Now I know the Lord works in mysterious ways, but this was beyond. I remember reading once that if you opened your refrigerator and found it filled with one thousand dollar bills, you would experience two simultaneous emotions. The first is the unbridled elation that your money problems are behind you. The second is the alarm that something doesn't compute in the natural universe.

That's what went through me. In a fractional second, I had four competing thoughts. The first was, "Oh thank God." The second was, "What is he doing here?" The third was that I should have had the courage to talk to him personally when we switched rabbis. And the fourth was that I shouldn't look a gift horse in the mouth five minutes before my wedding when the guy who was supposed to marry us was nowhere in sight.

Well, gut-check time. I pulled the rabbi aside and told him apologetically that we had elected to use someone else. To his credit (I guess this is the stuff that makes one a man of God), he was of good humor about the confusion. He wished me a wonderful day and a happy marriage, and gracefully departed. As if the universe were now satisfied that I had learned some profound lesson, Rabbi Kipnes materialized. After muttering something about the traffic problem in Los Angeles, he said, "Why don't we go sign the *ketubah* and get you two married."

Your mom's parents were too sick to travel, but otherwise we were surrounded by loving friends and family. Rabbi Kipnes infused the ceremony with warmth and affection, and when our friend Tisha sang an amazing rendition of "The First Time Ever I Saw Your Face," she brought down the house.

Now, my favorite custom in a Jewish wedding (other than kissing the bride) is when the groom breaks a glass with his foot. There are various explanations for this tradition, ranging from symbolizing the destruction of the Temple in Jerusalem, to symbolizing the taking of the bride's virginity (!), and even to humorously symbolizing the last time the husband can put his foot down. The one I like best, though, is that the broken glass reminds us of the fragility of marriage, and that both husband and wife must care for and nourish the relationship lest it shatter irreparably. Once the groom breaks the glass, everyone yells "*mazel tov*" and the ceremony ends.

As a practical matter, the groom breaks a very light crystal or, since the glass is hidden under a handkerchief, sometimes even a small light bulb. Both are easy to break, minimizing the risk of injury, and both make a loud popping sound for full effect. Unfortunately, the restaurant where we got married wasn't well versed in these realities. Instead, the restaurant provided one of its incredibly sturdy lead crystal water glasses. As a result, when the rabbi instructed me to break the glass and I pushed my right foot down, the glass did not break.

Instead of a hearty "*mazel tov*," the place erupted in uproarious, sustained laughter that would have been the envy of any comedian. Though it probably lasted less than a minute, in my embarrassment the laughter felt like forever. When it finally subsided, Rabbi Kipnes came to the rescue and said, "Because he loves her, he perseveres." This time I gave it everything I had, and the glass mercifully gave way. Everyone clapped and cheered and yelled "*mazel tov*," and your mom and I exited the *huppah* as husband and wife. Afterward we ate and danced deep into the night, and the highlight of the evening was when Jamie serenaded your mom and me with "From This Moment On" by Shania Twain.

And yes, our wedding day contained some life lessons too. The importance of facing our fears (and our rabbis) head-on. The importance of persevering in the face of adversity (and of strong glassware). And maybe most profoundly through the prism of time, that our lives are in fact storybooks, not dissimilar to the ones we read as children. It's just that along the way we encounter our own unique twists and turns. How we confront those twists and turns, and what we learn from them, weave the fabric of our stories and define the content of our character.

I look forward to watching your storybook continue to unfold, Mackenzie, and I owe you a letter for your wedding day too.

All my everlasting love,

Dad

YOUR GRANDMA AND ME AT THE EIFFEL TOWER WHEN I WAS A TEEN

# Nine: The Fragility of Life

Dear Mackenzie,

Sometimes you roll your eyes at me when I suggest that you spend more time with your sisters, or that you Skype with your aunt and uncle, or that you call your grandpa. At your age, collecting family memories to cherish later in life doesn't feel as important as, say, playing with your friend Bellah or downloading a new app. But it will.

On the afternoon of October 1, 2003, I left work early and headed to the City of Hope in Duarte, California, to donate platelets. All I knew about platelets is that they are cell fragments that circulate in the blood, that they have something to do with the blood's ability to clot, and that you need them to live.

I was queasy about the process, and since your aunt Viv is a nurse, I had asked her how donating platelets worked. She said the whole thing took about an hour and a half and, at least in those days, you could see the blood get pumped out of your arm, go through a machine, and then return to your body. I really didn't want to go through with it, but a friend's father was battling bone marrow cancer and donating platelets felt like a tangible way that I could help.

My cell phone rang as I pulled into the parking lot. Viv's number came up on the caller ID, but I was apprehensive enough without hearing another medical explanation, so I let the call go to voice mail. I figured I would call her back on the drive home, once the worst part of my day was over.

When I got back in the car a couple of hours later, I saw that Viv had called five or six more times. When I called her back, she was very distraught and told me that your grandma Sonia had been in a terrible car accident and that no one could locate her. My mind reeled. What did that even mean? For starters, if she had been in a car accident, wouldn't she be at the site of the crash?

Viv explained that your grandma belonged to a cultural group called the International Women Associates. Your grandma and twenty or so other women from that group had taken a day trip to a Japanese floral exhibit in Rockford, Illinois. On the way back to Chicago, a tractor-trailer had barreled into their tour bus on Interstate 90. A number of the women had died on impact, and more than a dozen others had been taken to various area hospitals. Viv said that from the little she had been able to garner, it appeared that your grandma was one of those.

She promised to keep calling around and said she would get back to me the moment she knew something. Your mom had already spoken to Viv by the time I reached her, and she was calling Chicago-area hospitals as well.

The drive back from the City of Hope took forever, and the radio silence from Viv made it even worse. Your grandma and grandpa had been divorced for many years by that time, but your grandpa had been a well-known physician in Chicago when he lived there, and he too was working the phones. No one seemed to know anything.

I didn't know what I could do, but I didn't feel comfortable doing nothing, so I decided to take a red eye to Chicago. You and your mom took me to the airport, and with my heart in my throat I got on the plane. I hoped that by the time I landed, I would be greeted with some good news.

Mackenzie, your grandma came from very humble beginnings. Your great-grandfather was an unsuccessful traveling salesman in Montevideo, Uruguay. They were dirt poor, and as I understand it your grandma had to drop out of high school to help support the family. She married your grandpa when she was twenty-three, and after Viv and I were born, our family immigrated to the United States in 1964.

Although your grandma had dropped out of high school, she never lost her thirst for knowledge. She spoke five languages fluently, and once your aunt Viv and I went off to college, your grandma went back to school too. She somehow finagled a high school diploma, and in her forties went to college and got both a B.A. and an M.A. degree in comparative literature. In her late fifties, your grandma earned a Ph.D. in sociology. That was one of the proudest achievements of her life.

We had seen your grandma just a few weeks before. She had flown to Los Angeles to help you celebrate your second birthday, and it was so much fun watching her and you play together. She had stayed at the Sofitel on Beverly Boulevard, which was your grandma's favorite hotel in Los Angeles. She loved the elegant rooms and the impeccable service, and most of all she savored the opportunity to speak French with the hotel staff.

The morning she was scheduled to fly home, I drove to the Sofitel to take her to the airport. I was waiting in the lobby when the elevator door opened and out stepped your grandma. She was wearing a bright red jacket and was pulling a small rolling suitcase behind her. She didn't immediately notice me, and she walked to the front desk to check out.

As I watched her from the doorway, I remember being taken with how regally she carried herself. She was so poised and confident, so comfortable in her own skin. That was no accident. Over the previous two decades, she had traveled the world as the Chicago executive director of an international organization called Alliance Française, which promotes the French language and culture. She had dined with kings and prime ministers. Her friends included diplomats, Nobel laureates, and many of the distinguished literati of Chicago. The palatial lobby of the Sofitel suited her, and I was filled with joy at how far her journey in life had taken her, from her ultrahumble beginnings to that moment.

As I flew to Chicago, I did the things I suspect most people do in these situations. I had imaginary conversations with your grandma. I made deals with God. I wondered how something so bad could happen literally as I was donating platelets to help someone else in need.

Unfortunately, my sweet daughter, when I landed the next morning, your aunt Viv delivered the news that your grandma Sonia had not survived. Her journey, at least in this life, was over.

You don't remember her since you were so young when she died, but over time we hope to tell you lots of great stories about her. What you should know is that your grandma loved you with all her heart. She was so happy to have you in the world and in her life. And as she looks down from heaven, she must be bursting with joy and pride at the wonderful young person you've become.

Now go call someone you care about and tell them you love them.

All my everlasting love,

Dad

# Ten: The Importance of Failure

Dear Mackenzie,

Every so often someone will think it's a good idea to give your mom or me unsolicited advice on how we should be raising you. Interestingly, it's often someone who doesn't have kids of his or her own, and even more often the advice comes on the heels of your being overly active (read: obnoxious) in a public place.

On some level I can appreciate that. We've all been there. Yet unless someone observes us engaging in behavior that would warrant calling family services, my visceral instinct is that how we raise you is personal to us, good intentions notwithstanding.

I've similarly learned to keep my opinions to myself when I observe other parents doing or saying things differently than I would. Not long ago I overheard a friend of mine tell his young son that he was "absolutely perfect" and that "everything he did was perfect." He's a great young kid for sure. But if he's indeed perfect, that trait alone would separate him from the rest of humanity.

I should have kept my mouth shut and I knew it, but I couldn't help myself. I asked my friend if indeed he felt his son was perfect. My friend looked at me like I was crazy and replied that the boy was anything but perfect, but that he wanted to create in him an expectation of success. I then asked if he didn't worry that planting the notion of perfection would inhibit his son from trying things he feared he might not do perfectly. The look my friend gave me was my cue to change the subject, but I got to thinking about the best way to create an expectation of success in you.

The problem with telling people that they are perfect as a way to program them for success is that success has little if anything to do with perfection. On the contrary, success usually follows imperfection and failure. That doesn't mean I want you to be comfortable with failure. I don't. I hope you'll have the same visceral antipathy toward it that I have. At the same time I hope you won't fear failure, and that you'll understand and embrace its role in getting to success.

I'm not suggesting that my friend should be drilling imperfection or failure into his son. What I am suggesting is that you give yourself permission to search for your holy grail by embracing your imperfections and by being willing to consistently risk failure. That's the true road map to both success and happiness.

You don't know who Michael Jordan is, but maybe by the time you read this letter you will. He was probably the greatest basketball player to ever put on a uniform. Here's what Michael Jordan said about success and failure: "I've missed more than 9,000 shots in my career. I've lost almost 300 games. Twenty-six times I've been trusted to take the game-winning shot and missed. I've failed over and over and over again in my life. And that's why I succeed."

Some of my own spectacular failures have led to my greatest adventures, which in hindsight I realize have enriched me greatly. I spent a number of years in a self-imposed career purgatory. I left the entertainment industry in the middle of my ascent to "experience life." I traveled around the country as part of Bill Clinton's first presidential campaign. I worked for the World Cup when the men's games were in the United States. I sat second chair on a murder case. I even worked for a San Francisco based environmental group, lobbying local municipalities. What did I know about that? Absolutely nothing. I was chasing experiences, not success. I got the former in spades. The latter? Not so much.

In fact, my sweet daughter, the most honest thing I can tell you is that eventually my career in the entertainment industry plummeted. Additionally, bouncing around from experience to experience, I ran out of savings and amassed a crazy amount of credit-card debt. I finally reached a crossroads where I feared if I didn't get back on track then, I never would. My friend Nick LaTerza used to joke that my career was in its "last call" stage.

By the time I wanted to return to the entertainment industry, it no longer seemed to want me. My friends in the business didn't believe I really wanted to "settle down" into one career. Or they thought I was too old to start over. Or whatever. The point is, no one would hire me.

In those days I often went running at Venice Beach. One day as I ran, my spirits were dreadfully low. I had just gotten my umpteenth rejection from who knows where, and I remember thinking that I had ruined my life.

I remember thinking that I would never get another opportunity to make something of myself. I had no idea how I would support myself or a family. I chastised myself for chasing rainbows and for tilting at windmills. I ran and ran, until I finally cried myself out. I must have been quite a sight as I railed to myself, though in the circus that is Venice Beach, it's possible no one even gave me a second look.

By the grace of God, a month or two and a hundred rejections later I got a job at a talent agency called Writers and Artists, and started the long climb back. That limbo period of my career was flooded with false moves, failure, and insecurity. Yet those days were some of my most interesting and memorable ones. The lessons I learned from those experiences—resourcefulness, resilience, tenacity, compassion for the underdog—made me a better executive and a better person than I might otherwise have become.

In the end, Mackenzie, failure is simply an event, not a state of being. The best way for you to maximize the probability of success is to approach what you do with a commitment to excellence, with a strong work ethic, with integrity, and with passion for the task at hand. The rest is just background noise.

And if you make that process your constant companion, once in a blue moon you may even get a taste of that soul-enriching, heart-thumping, head-swelling, fleeting event called—dare I say it—perfection.

All my everlasting love,

Dad

# Eleven:
# Wolves, Demons, and Other Monsters

Dear Mackenzie,

You've had a lot of success in the entertainment industry at a very young age, and people often ask me how I feel about your being an actor. I answer that I'm excited for you. I say that in my experience, it's very hard to find something one is passionate about in life, let alone at your age, and the fact that you're doing well is a bonus.

I also acknowledge that having seen firsthand the ups and downs that artists endure, and how difficult that life can be, I am conflicted at the same time. I add that this is not the childhood I would necessarily have chosen for you.

The truth, though, is that most days I don't feel particularly conflicted. You love what you do. I see how much you enjoy auditioning, being on a set or on a stage, going to premieres, and being on red carpets. What's there to be conflicted about? Thus I get lulled into a false sense of security. But every so often the conflict and the dread I do feel about your having a life in the arts hits me upside the head like a two-by-four.

When I was starting my career in the early 1980s, several of my clients were recording artists in the R&B world. I remember at some point the town started to buzz that Clive Davis, the legendary head of Arista Records at the time, had discovered yet another singing sensation, this one with roots in the gospel world.

In those days MTV was an actual music channel and played music videos around the clock. One day a video came on for a song called "How Will I Know," and the singer took my breath away. She was beautiful. She exuded a playful sex appeal, and her voice was radiant. Her name was Whitney Houston. She burst onto the scene and into the American consciousness and became a big star almost overnight.

I met Whitney Houston only once. It was early in her career, and she couldn't have been more than twenty-two or twenty-three years old. I was at some industry event with a client whose own career at the time was even more nascent than Whitney's. My client noticed her across the room, and said she wanted to meet her.

This was long before bodyguards and entourages and Bobby Brown came into Whitney's life, and I went and introduced myself. I told her that the firm where I had first worked after law school represented her cousin Dionne Warwick, and that one of my very first assignments had been to drive to Ms. Warwick's house with some legal documents for her to sign. I said that Ms. Warwick was the first star I had ever met, and that afterward I had called my parents back home to tell them that their son was now officially in show business.

Whitney was very gracious and she, my client, and I all chatted for a while that night. From then on I watched from afar as she became a huge recording artist, and then a movie star as well. As time went by I also watched as she struggled with her addictions and her personal demons. Her instrument deteriorated and her career struggled as she abused her body and her psyche.

On the day of her death we were all discussing Whitney at dinner, and you said you didn't know who she was or why she was famous. Sometime when you have a chance, my sweet daughter, you should experience the transcendent talent she possessed.

Watch the video that launched her into superstardom. Savor her soulful renditions of "My Love Is Your Love," "I Will Always Love You," the national anthem (believe it or not), or any of the other hits that led her to become one of the biggest-selling recording artists of all time. See her star turn in *the Bodyguard*.

I was sad when I read of her untimely death. And I got a terrible pain in my stomach thinking about you in this industry, and of all the minefields that can explode on you if you're not careful.

As I write you this letter, no one knows exactly what caused Whitney Houston's death, but it's likely that her demons and addictions played a role. I suspect every artist views her passing the same way NFL athletes look on when another player is paralyzed or otherwise severely injured during a game. They regard it with sympathy and sadness for a fallen comrade, and with the unspoken but very real knowledge that "there but for the grace of God go I."

It turns out, Mackenzie, that in fact I'm profoundly conflicted. I want you to do what you love. I want you to succeed at it. I want you to buck convention. Yet at the same time, I'm frightened for you when I see how many people get overtaken by the volatile mix of adulation and rejection that are part of an artist's experience. The wolf at the door and the personal demons lie in wait side by side.

I pray that your mom and I can help keep you grounded and happy. I pray that (to paraphrase Rudyard Kipling) you can treat those two impostors called triumph and disaster just the same. I pray that no one with character deficiencies like some of those who were in Whitney's circle ever finds his or her way into your life or into your heart.

So I will continue to support your artistry. I will continue to delight in your successes. I will continue to be the best father I can be and to hug you as often as you will let me. And though I'll try not to show it, I will continue to worry about you and to ask whatever higher power is out there that wolves, demons, and other monsters stay away from my little girl.

All my everlasting love,

Dad

# Twelve: Faith and Religion

Dear Mackenzie,

Your mom and I are not particularly religious in a conventional sense, and we've been grappling with how best to give you a proper religious education.

Faith, prayer, and invocation are crucial elements of the human experience, and we understand their importance. But how to best inculcate faith and religion into your life? Is it through organized religion? We certainly want you to learn the Jewish customs and traditions with which we grew up, and will try to teach them to you. But is that the only path to God?

Your aunt Viv and I grew up in a very nonreligious household. Yes, we went to temple and I went to Hebrew school, but in hindsight that seemed geared more toward community and tradition than toward communion with God.

Once when I was about your age, your grandma baked a cake during Passover. When she brought it to the dinner table, I was horrified. I told her she was not supposed to cook with any leavening agents during Passover and accused her of "not being Jewish."

Your grandma was nonplussed. She replied that though she had no idea it was Passover, she was indeed Jewish to the core. Being the headstrong kid that I was, I didn't believe her at the time and I demanded she throw the cake away. Now that I no longer attend Sunday School, I can't keep track of a single Jewish holiday either, yet still consider myself profoundly Jewish. It's just one of the many apologies I owe your grandma!

By the way, Mackenzie, your grandma almost shut down my Bar Mitzvah. A week or two before the ceremony, your aunt Viv and I got in a big fight, as young siblings sometimes do, and apparently I called her some very nasty names. Your grandma was quite upset with me. She said if that was how I interacted with others when I was angry, I was not ready to be a man, either under Jewish law or any other. I don't remember how I got it all back on track, but I sure remember the lesson.

While I was in college, I studied comparative religions and came away confused and conflicted, not only about Judaism, but about all organized religions. How could so many religions have such conflicting narratives? And which one was right?

The God I knew and trusted was that of the Old Testament. Yet the God I studied when I read the New Testament struck me as kinder and more loving (1 Corinthians 13 is a good example) than the God I had studied as a kid in Sunday School (the complete destruction of Jericho, Sodom and Gomorrah, and of the Amalekites comes to mind).

The New Testament confused me too. It teaches that Jesus is the Son of God and part of the Holy Trinity, and that He died for our sins. But the New Testament also teaches that unless one accepts both that Jesus is the Son of God and that He died for our sins, one cannot be absolved and enter the kingdom of heaven. How can that be? If Jesus is God, would He demand, or even allow, that we must believe Him to be God in order to be saved? I inadvertently started quite a heated discussion in class when I suggested that the notion seemed more like the human foible of vanity than anything particularly holy.

Then there's the Book of Mormon (no, not the Broadway musical), which if I remember correctly teaches that there may be multiple gods, and that God the Father has a wife. And I don't know much about Buddhism, but I do remember being taught that in order to embrace Buddhism one must deny Christ, and the Bible too. Hmmm.

I've heard Hinduism described as a conglomeration of distinct philosophical views rather than a rigid common set of beliefs. That, of course, is completely in oppositon to the teachings of both Judaism and Christianity. And though I don't know very much about Islam, or the Bahai faith, or the Swedenborgian Church, or some of the various other religions around the world, I know enough to be aware that many of their teachings don't line up with those of other religions.

Is one of these right and all the others wrong? Does an invocation by a Sikh address a different higher power than that of a Christian? Does an invocation by a Jain address a different higher power than that of a Jew? I find that hard to fathom. And it seems improbable that any one religious belief system is more or less valid than any other.

Which brings us to faith. Faith is belief that is not based on proof. Faith is knowing that the hand of God, however we choose to define it, is there to help guide us and keep us from harm even if we can't see it.

I was never able to visualize or articulate what the hand of God meant until you started to walk. You were just a toddler, and you would walk for a bit and then fall down. Then you'd get yourself back up and try again. Walk. Fall down. Get up. Repeat.

Your mom and I started to follow you around the house with our arms outstretched, ready to step in if terrible harm seemed imminent. We didn't want you to know we were doing that, though. If you turned around to look at us, we'd pretend to be doing something else. Yet we kept a watchful eye and our arms ready on your behalf. On a larger scale, that is how I now envision the hand of God in all of our lives.

So which organized religion got it right? I don't know. What I do know is that faith and religion are important, that we'll guide you as best we can, and that ultimately you'll have to determine for yourself what makes the most sense for you. The good news is that stripped of their different narratives, virtually all religions boil down to the same basic precepts, designed to make our lives richer and to move the human race forward:

Have a kind heart.

Treat others the way you would want them to treat you (the Golden Rule).

Be charitable to those less fortunate.

Take care of your family and your neighbor.

Love learning.

Have faith in a higher power.

If you follow those basic tenets throughout your life, Mackenzie, you won't go wrong, no matter what religion ultimately speaks to your heart, mind, and soul.

And that, my sweet daughter, is the gospel according to Norman.

All my everlasting love in this kingdom and beyond,

Dad

# Thirteen: Daddy-Sitting

Dear Mackenzie,

Parenting is hard.

In 2012 in Houston, Texas, a mother of ten children threw a birthday party at the local Chuck E. Cheese's for her five-year-old daughter and then left her at the restaurant.

The good news is that she didn't do it on purpose. The bad news is that she didn't realize her mistake until 8:00 AM the following day, when she was getting her other nine kids ready for school. Fortunately the child was fine, and the police said they planned to analyze the surveillance video to decide whether or not criminal charges were warranted.

No doubt the event was traumatic for the little girl, though hopefully she won't remember much of it as time goes by. And certainly the police should take these matters seriously. Yet I have little doubt that if I had ten children to look after, I would periodically forget one or another of them all over the city. At the very least.

Once when you were six, your mom went to Cleveland to visit her best friend Suzy. It was the first time I had been called upon to take care of you alone for any length of time. I was excited to have a whole weekend of bonding time with you, but I was a little anxious too. What if something came up that I couldn't handle?

Your mom assured me that she was just a phone call away. She also reminded me that I could always call Jamie, who was living nearby on the USC campus. I chided your mom for implying that our college-age daughter might have been better equipped to handle a child care issue than I was, but secretly I took comfort that Jamie was indeed there if I got in over my head.

In those days you took a dance class every Friday night at a dance studio in North Hollywood called Millennium. That Friday I took great care to dress you in the outfit Mom had set out for you before she left. I made sure you had your water, your dance bag, and your dance shoes, just as your mom had instructed. I triple-checked the time of the class so you wouldn't be late, and I made us leave for class way too early in case we hit traffic. When we got there, the parking gods smiled on us and we got a spot right inside the Millennium lot. So far, so good.

After class, we decided to make a night of it, and I suggested we walk to the pizza place down the street. I was delighted at how smoothly things were going and quite proud of myself. What I didn't realize was that Millennium locked its parking lot at night, and when we returned from dinner we couldn't get to our car.

You got scared and started to cry, which is when my respect for your mother's parenting skills increased exponentially. Suddenly I was scared too, but for a different reason. I knew we could simply take a taxi home and get the car in the morning. That wasn't the problem. The problem was that I had no idea how to comfort you.

I put on my happiest face and told you this would be a fun adventure for the two us to share. I said that Mom would be very jealous when she heard we got to take a taxi ride together. That seemed to pacify you a little, so I decided not to mention that I had left the house keys inside the car and thus had no clue how we'd get in the house once we got there.

Jamie had a key, and I called her on the cab ride home. You were being quite brave, but you were still sniffling when I got Jamie's voice mail, so I made a point of being very jovial as I left her a message. Unfortunately, when you heard the part about my not having the house keys, you started bawling again.

Like most people of her generation, Jamie rarely listens to her voice mails, so I covered my bases and sent her a text as well. Yet by the time the taxi arrived at home, Jamie had not returned either my call or my text.

Plan B was for me to jump over the gate, but you were now crying for a third time and begged me not to leave you alone outside the gate. I didn't know what to do. I told you that nothing bad could ever happen to you as long as we were together, and that I'd have the gate open and be back in no time. When that didn't calm you, I told you to count while I went over the gate. I promised that I'd give you a dollar for every number you got to before I was back.

Yes, that's pathetic. I admit it. But twelve dollars and a bruised knee later, we were at least inside the property, and we caught a break when a glass door to the family room had been left unlocked. We were home at last.

Mackenzie, you could not have been more adorable or courageous that night. I suggested you write Mom a note about your bravery for her to read upon her return, and after some chocolate pudding and twenty minutes of cuddling, you fell asleep in my arms. I was still a little in shock about how the evening had unfolded when Jamie finally called in. "What's up?" she asked innocently.

The next morning you told Mom about my first solo flight as a parent, adding that "Daddy-sitting" wasn't as easy as you had expected. For my part, I told your mom to please hurry home.

By the way, a couple of weeks ago you told me that for a dad, I wasn't being very smart about something. You had a big smile on your face. I thought that was an interesting comment, and I asked you what I wasn't being smart about. You explained that I had told you I didn't want you to read these "letters to Mackenzie" until you were eighteen, but that since I was posting the letters online you could read them at any time.

Well, that was certainly a point well taken. I asked if you had indeed read the letters. "No, Daddy," you scolded me. "You told me not to."

You then asked me why you couldn't read the letters until you were an adult and if there was something bad in the letters. I replied that on the contrary, the letters grew out of my profound love for you, but that given some of the themes in the letters, you might savor them more as an adult.

I could see the wheels turning in your head, and then another big smile crossed your face. "Daddy," you said, "will you write me a letter I can read now?"

Yes, my sweet daughter. Here it is.

All my everlasting love,

Dad

# Fourteen: Peer Pressure

Dear Mackenzie,

You're way too young to have studied Shakespeare, but by the time you read this letter, Polonius's famous admonition to his son in *Hamlet*, "To thine own self be true," may be familiar to you. As I recall, Polonius was actually telling his son to look after his own interests, but fortunately the phrase has evolved over time into something more profound.

These days, being true to yourself means following your own path rather than the path others would have you follow. More important for you as you head into your teens, it means holding on to your core values even in the face of pressure to do otherwise.

Our core principles are important. They guide how we live our lives, how we comport ourselves, and how we interact with those around us. Honesty. Kindness. Loyalty. It's all pretty straightforward.

Fitting in is important too. The need to belong is universal and hardwired. We all want and deserve to be part of the in-crowd, at least once in a while. And whether we like it or not, we all feel like outsiders once in a while too.

So what is it about group dynamics that so often pits belonging against our principles? I don't know the science behind it, but I bet that deep in our subconscious minds it has something to do with what happened when the Neanderthal tribes met our Cro-Magnon ancestors a hundred thousand years ago. Being different got you killed.

Today being different doesn't necessarily get you killed, but it often gets you ostracized, especially as a young adult. In my high school days, you were susceptible to being made fun of if you wore glasses ("four-eyes"), or if you wore braces ("metal-mouth"), or if you were straitlaced ("dork"), or if you did well in school ("nerd"). And those were the more innocent ones!

I wish I could tell you, my sweet daughter, that you'll never be tempted to compromise your values simply to fit in. But in truth you certainly will. What's worse, life and the human condition being what they are, you'll probably be tested when you're at your most vulnerable and when your need to feel accepted will be the strongest.

I wish I could tell you that if you hold firm to your principles in those moments, the group members will embrace your fortitude, realize the error of their ways, and hold you in high esteem. Unfortunately the opposite is far more likely. You may find their guns retrained on you as the target of their ridicule.

And I wish I could tell you that if that happens, the courage you'll have exhibited will at least make you feel great about yourself, that you'll realize those who would ask you to compromise your values are not real friends, and that you'll also realize those who would have you participate in making someone feel bad are not worthy of you.

Well, that actually will be the case, although it won't happen right away. First you'll feel alienated and betrayed. You'll wonder why you stood your ground and you'll wonder if it was worth it. You'll feel certain that no one would have done the same for you. Though those dark thoughts will seem very real to you at the time, they are not. They are fleeting impostors.

In those difficult moments you must have faith in and hold tight to your core beliefs. For if you do, after a while your spirit will once again take flight and you'll understand that not fitting in can sometimes be a blessing. But you've known that from a very young age, Mackenzie.

A few years ago, when you were in second grade, you came home from school one day and told us you had learned about cigarettes and the health dangers they pose. You were articulate and passionate on the subject, and your mom and I were duly impressed.

Being the willful young person you are, you set about on a mission of pointing out every smoker you saw, whether you knew them or not, and urging your mom and me to discuss their unsafe habit with them. Even your sister Jamie, who I hope will not be a smoker by the time you read this (hint, hint, Jamie) started sneaking around to steal her puffs lest she incur your wrath.

You went to such an extreme that your mom and I started to worry you might start confronting strangers directly. We didn't think an adult would take kindly to being chastised by a seven-year-old, even if your intentions were noble.

One night around that time period I had a business dinner at the Havana Club, a well-known restaurant and cigar club in Beverly Hills. Over the course of dinner and drinks, everyone indulged, and when I arrived home I apparently reeked of cigars.

You were outraged, and asked me if I had smoked as well. The easy answer was no, but I didn't want to lie to you, so I admitted that I had. You were very disappointed in me, which I have to say broke my heart, and you asked me why I had done it. The truth is that I enjoy a good cigar now and again, but that answer clearly wasn't going to cut it with you just then. So I said that since everyone at the table was smoking, I had a cigar as well. "That's no excuse," you countered, as indignant as any seven-year-old I've ever seen. "And if you were getting peer pressure from your friends, you should have gotten up and left the restaurant."

Shakespeare himself couldn't have said that any better.

All my everlasting love,

Dad

# Fifteen: Marriage

Dear Mackenzie,

*"If love is blind and marriage is an institution, then marriage is an institution for the blind."*
     —James Graham

*"Losing a wife can be very hard. In my case it was nearly impossible."*
     —Henny Youngman

Why are there so many dumb jokes about marriage? What's the institution of marriage really like?

Shortly before your mom and I got married, I asked your aunt Viv for a straight answer to that very question. She had been married a number of years by that time. She also knew that like many males in Los Angeles, I had a tendency to run away from commitment. "Marriage is not always fun," she said, "and it's not always easy. But it's always worthwhile."

My grandpa Goldberg, your great-grandfather, was born in Austria, or maybe Poland, in 1894, and Granny Goldberg was born in Poland in 1900. At that time in many parts of Europe, marriages were still arranged. No one in our immediate family remembers with certainty, but I believe their marriage was indeed an arranged one. I do know they married very young.

My grandfather had grandiose dreams, and sometime around 1920 he tried to immigrate to America. The quota system at the time kept him out of the United States, so he decided to move to South America instead. As was the custom in those days, my grandfather went ahead alone, promising my grandmother that once he settled and found a job she would join him.

The story I've heard over the years is that when my grandfather got to Uruguay, he met another woman and fell in love. Torn between duty and love, my grandfather chose duty. He brought my grandmother to Montevideo, where they had a long and apparently unhappy marriage.

Not long after my grandfather died, my paternal grandparents told me a heartbreaking story. After the funeral, a number of people were sharing memories of your great-grandfather. Everyone was recounting how he had loved his daughter (your grandma), how he had loved your aunt Viv and me, and so on. And finally Granny Goldberg started to weep and said, "Yes, he loved everyone in the world except me."

What a terrible, terrible weight with which to be burdened througout a lifetime of marriage. I can't begin to imagine how my grandmother must have felt; a young woman filled with life and hope, leaving her friends and family behind to follow her husband to a distant new world, only to find or suspect once she got there that her husband loved someone else.

Remember that this was almost a hundred years ago. Today both would have had more choices available to them and quite probably it would all have gone down very differently. Yet marriage remains as challenging as ever. In an age when divorce is not the social stain it once was, it's even more unusual for two people to be willing to grow together while giving each other the room to find individual fulfillment.

Marriage isn't perfect. Sometimes I jump up and down wanting acknowledgement or attention from your mom but she's too exhausted by the challenges of her day. It drives me nuts. Sometimes your mom needs me to be there for her and simply listen, and I don't answer the bell. It drives her nuts. Sometimes we get angry at each other. Sometimes we pout. Well, I pout.

These days temptation threatens to derail marriages more than ever, and there are more opportunities than ever to act on those temptations. When times are tough, pulling the ripcord can feel a lot easier than staying to fight for the relationship.

Studies have shown that half of all first marriages end in divorce, that two-thirds of second marriages end in divorce, and that three-quarters of third marriages end in divorce. Fourth marriages? Fuggedaboutit. So why stay?

Well, my sweet daughter, everyone who stays married does so for different reasons. You'll no doubt have your own. For me, I stay because your mom is my best friend. I stay because your mom is the one person in the world I trust with my very life. I stay because I miss her when we're apart. I stay because I feel whole when we're together. I stay because whether we're swinging from the chandeliers or changing a light bulb in a chandelier, there's no one with whom I'd rather do either.

Herbert and Zelmyra Fisher hold the Guinness world record for the longest marriage in history. Before Mr. Fisher died in 2011, he and his wife were married for eighty-six years. Asked the secret to the longevity of their marriage, Mrs. Fisher replied modestly that sometimes "God ties great knots."

Not too long ago your aunt Viv got very, very sick. She spent almost two months in the hospital, which in this day and age is unusual and dangerous. Things got a lot worse before they got better. When she was finally out of the woods, I spoke with her about her experience. Among other things, Viv told me she didn't think she would have made it through without your uncle Ron.

She said Ron stood like a rock for her throughout the entire ordeal. He took care of the kids and the house. He worked a full-time job. He navigated the doctors, managed the family dynamics, and still found the time and energy to spend hours at the hospital looking after her.

Viv said that during the previous few months she had come to understand in a very profound way what marriage is really about. She said that if for the rest of their lives together Ron never again held her hand, or bought her flowers, or even told her that he loved her, Ron's love for her and for the sanctity of their marriage would nonetheless be forever ingrained in her heart.

For your aunt Viv, that's the good news. The even better news for Viv is that a spouse who stands anchored like that during a terribly low point in your life is also likely to keep holding your hand, and to keep buying you flowers, and to keep telling you he loves you.

In the end that's the kind of marriage we all want and deserve, and the kind of marriage your mom and I wish for you.

All my everlasting love,

Dad

# Sixteen: The Great Beyond

Dear Mackenzie,

A good friend of mine just lost her significant other. He was only fifty years old when he died, and he left behind a five-year-old son. It's a very sad situation.

The other day my friend posted a few pictures of their family on Facebook as a memorial, and two of the pictures in particular really touched my heart. The first was of the little boy wearing some kind of worker vest or fishing vest. His dad was kneeling next to him as the two read what looked to be directions for something. Maybe they were assembling a piece of furniture together, or maybe they were getting ready to go fishing. I'm not sure, and the specifics don't matter. Whatever they were doing, the picture gave me a glimpse of a father bonding with and teaching his son.

The second picture was even more gripping. According to the caption, it was taken just a few days before the boy's father passed away. In it, the little boy is lying on top of his dad and the two are hugging each other for dear life as they both look up at the camera. In a different context, the image would have been wonderfully heartwarming.

The boy's father had been very ill and may have known he was nearing the end. As I looked at these very moving images, I started thinking about you and me. I wondered what might have gone through my own mind as a parent if I had lain dying when you were only five and I had the chance to hug you as a little girl one final time. Would this last moment of intimacy have to carry the two of us through all eternity?

Like most people, sometimes I wish I knew what happens to us after our time on this earth is done. When we go to that great beyond, where exactly are we going? What is the next kingdom we hear so much about? Is there life after death? Is there reincarnation? Is the soul truly immortal? Will we be able to keep a watchful and loving eye on our loved ones from up above? We have more questions than answers, to say the least.

The last question troubles me the most. Jamie and Heather are now fully formed adults. Of course your mom and I want to savor them, help them, hang out with them, and share experiences with them for many years to come. But at least I take some comfort that irrespective of me or your mom, Heather and Jamie are positioned going forward to make their way in the world just fine.

It's a little different with you, my sweet daughter. Although we often joke that you're ten going on twenty-five, in the end you're not yet fully developed or able to fend for yourself. You still have a lot to learn cognitively and emotionally. Your mom and I want to be here to protect you and teach you, and naturally we plan to.

But what if we couldn't be here for you? My fervent prayer is that Heather, Jamie, and other family and friends would step in and you'd end up just fine. But would your mom and I be able to help you, or guide you, or experience you in any way from the other side?

Virtually every religion addresses the notion of an afterlife that encompasses either reincarnation, the immortality of the soul, or both. Historians, theologians, philosophers, and other people much smarter than I have been debating the afterlife, or the possible lack of it, for thousands of years. There are more explanations and theories about what happens after we die than you can imagine. They're all equally likely or unlikely depending on your faith, your hopes, and your spiritual needs.

The theory I would most like to be true is that when my time on earth is done, I would be able to look upon you, your sisters, and the rest of our family and recognize our connection.

I guess that's an earthly yearning and not a spiritual one. Maybe in the end our spirit is infinitely more evolved than that. Sometimes I feel your grandma's presence with me, and she's been gone almost a decade. I'll remember something she said to me that makes me smile. Or I'll be feeling down and the memory of her will pop into my head and cheer me up. But is that really your grandma reaching out from some other place, or is it simply memory association here on earth?

Many years ago, the night Granny Goldberg (your great-grandmother) died, I had an overwhelming feeling as I drifted into a fitful sleep. It was as if her spirit were urging me to come with her and I was trying to get out of my body to follow. It scared the bejesus out of me, and that night I barely slept for fear that if I fell asleep I might die. The sensation was all too real. But was the spirit world really beckoning me, or were my heart and brain simply grappling with the notion of losing my grandma, with whom I had been very close? I have no idea.

Here's what I do know. Life is fragile. Our time is short.

Any given hug could be our last.

If there is a great beyond, I hope I can recognize you in it. Until then, I will love you in the here and now and count my blessings every day.

All my everlasting love,

Dad

# Seventeen: Art in the World

Dear Mackenzie,

Just as I marvel at your grandfather's musical gifts, I'm amazed by your acting and singing accomplishments at such a young age. Your aunt Viv was an accomplished musician when she was younger also, but if indeed creativity is genetic, I acknowledge that other than perhaps writing these letters to you, the artistic gene seems to have eluded me.

Ironically that's the very reason I got into the entertainment industry, and maybe even the secret of my success. I know how hard it is for artists, no matter how talented, to bring their gifts into being. I also know that the skill set and even the personality required to create art are often at odds with the skill set required to expose that art to the world. So take a person who understands that difference, maybe not that gifted but appreciative of the beauty and emotional power that great art brings to the world, sprinkle in a pinch of the "gift of gab," and voilà, I have a career.

I try not to forget that what I do is a noble calling. I try not to forget that my gift is playing a role in furthering the careers of some wonderful actors, writers, and directors. Katherine Heigl and the late James Gandolfini possessed extraordinary, God-given gifts, and they both had an absolute commitment to their crafts. I had nothing to do with those things. But when they thanked me in their acceptance speeches upon winning their Emmys, I felt like they were sharing a small piece of their immortality with me, and that was incredibly gratifying.

All of that said, having worked in the industry a long time, I periodically find myself numb to the miracle of creativity. In the daily grind, it's easy to forget why I wanted to get into show business in the first place. And that's exactly how I was feeling one Monday night as I made my way down to the storied nightclub in the West Village called The Bitter End.

For the past twenty-two years, on the first Monday of each month, The Bitter End transforms into a musical showcase for singers and songwriters called the New York Songwriters Circle. Famous songwriters and up-and-comers alike celebrate great original songs together, and perform them for each other in an intimate setting.

The Songwriters Circle is run by a wonderful singer-songwriter named Tina Shafer. Tina is a true artist, and she also happens to be one of my dearest friends dating back to our college days. Admittedly she looks much younger than I do, but whatever.

I was fully prepared to be unimpressed as I walked into the club. My goal was simply to sit through the performances and then go have a nice dinner with Tina. Instead, I was treated to an exhilarating reminder of the joy I still feel when I watch talented artists create. The burdens of my day evaporated as the various musicians held sway on stage, and my love for the arts was unexpectedly rekindled.

One of the performers that night was Tina's fifteen-year-old son, Ari, who is a prodigious musical talent in his own right. I observed Tina assess Ari on stage with a mixture of detached professional respect coupled with the beaming pride unique to a parent. Which of course made me think about you and your art. You go to auditions with unbridled excitement no matter what may have happened in the last one. You act alongside a great actor like Edie Falco on *Nurse Jackie*, and rather than being overwhelmed, you're delighted and in your element. You sing Broadway show tunes and no doubt imagine yourself on those stages. In short, my sweet daughter, you are an artist.

At the end of the show, Tina came back onstage one last time, and sang a song she cowrote with the late Phoebe Snow called "Above the Band." The song is an anthem to having a voice both in the world and in the arts. I asked Tina if I could reprint the lyrics for you, and she graciously agreed. Whether your life keeps you acting or takes you elsewhere, I hope these words one day remind you, as they did me, of the power of the creative arts.

*Stay clear*
*Stay focused*
*Create a little*
*Stay sober*
*Steady*
*And a little bit sane*
*Stay alive to survive*
*Past your fifteen minutes*
*Maybe someone will remember your name*
*Be a force for some good*
*Be a flame eternal*
*Be brave*
*Take risks*
*Have a thick skin*
*And even when all they see is external*
*Let your soul shine from within*
*Create an illusion*
*A small sleight of hand*
*Amidst the confusion*
*Rise up*
*Take command*
*And they'll hear you above the band*
*This old world keeps on turning*
*This life hangs on for the weak and strong*
*Even in the face of darkest evil*
*I believe that hope holds on*
*Dream big*
*Seek truth*
*Grab your moment*

*Find peace in the craziness of each day*
*I won't always be there to guide you*
*But I believe you're going to find your way*
*Create an illusion*
*A small sleight of hand*
*Amidst the confusion*
*Rise up*
*Make a stand*
*And they'll hear you above the band*
*Yes they will hear you above the band*
—"Above the Band," by Tina Shafer and Phoebe Snow

All my everlasting love,

Dad

MY BEST FRIEND, AND MY BEST MAN

# Eighteen: Friendship

Dear Mackenzie,

Nothing beats having a best friend.

Throughout the course of your life, you'll meet lots of people and call many of them friends. Some friendships will be short-lived and some will be long-lasting. You'll have some fair-weather friends and some who will stay beside you in rough waters. That's just how it goes. What I wish for you, my sweet daughter, is that at some point you'll experience a friendship like the one I had with Jeff Greer.

I met Jeff my first week of college at Case Western Reserve University. I walked into his dorm room late one night, told him with a bit of a swagger that I was planning to run for freshman class president, and asked for his vote. Jeff told me in no uncertain terms that I couldn't have it. When I asked him why, he said he too was running for freshman class president and intended to vote for himself.

A few hours, a few beers, and a few Phillies cigarillos later, we decided that maybe we could be better together than separate, and that we should run as a ticket for class president and vice president. Since I was the local Cleveland boy, I would run for president, and he, the New England transplant, would run for VP. That night, a small political dynasty was born at our school. More wonderfully, that night gave birth to a profound friendship between Jeff and me that lasted more than thirty-five years.

Jeff had a beautiful mind. He was intelligent. He had a great sense of humor. He had an uncanny ability to explore an issue from all sides. He loved people. And he had a deep personal moral code and sense of justice.

During our college years, Jeff and I were virtually inseparable. We ran student government together. We trolled the student union together. We partied together. We traveled together. We came close to being arrested together (don't ask). Everything seemed possible during those heady, exuberant days.

After college we didn't see each other as much. I went to California and Jeff went to New England, and then to Florida, and then back to New England. But our friendship remained strong. We'd go through periods when we talked all the time, and then sometimes we wouldn't talk for two or three years at a time.

The miracle of our friendship was that we could go several years without talking, and then one of us would call the other and it was like we'd just seen each other yesterday. We'd talk about politics and about sports and about our lives. Our respective paths could not have taken us to more different corners, and yet we savored each other's experiences as if they were our own.

Jeff called me once, shortly after he and his wife, Nancy, got married. Or maybe just after they had started dating seriously; I don't remember the exact time line. In any event, Jeff was living in Providence and working for the governor of Rhode Island, while Nancy was living in Washington, D.C., or traveling a lot to D.C. for work, or something like that.

All I remember is that they were apart a lot and it was troubling Jeff. He was concerned that the distance and time apart were hurting their relationship. "Jeff, you guys love each other very much," I told him. "I'm sure you'll be able to withstand some periods of separation."

"Look at us," I added. "Sometimes we don't even talk for years at a time, and our bond is as strong as ever."

"But unlike us," Jeff replied without missing a beat, "Nancy is beautiful, intelligent, and charming. She has many more options than you and I do."

About two years ago, Mackenzie, you were in New England with the Broadway tour of *Annie*, and Jeff and his wife came to see you in the show. They were so tickled watching you onstage, and we got to spend a wonderful weekend with them.

Nancy and your mom were good sports, and pretended to be interested while Jeff and I reminisced about the good old days for the umpteenth time. We even had dinner with Jeff's folks, who had been a second set of parents to me when Jeff and I were in college. I remember telling your mom that weekend how amazing it was to me that after all those years and all those miles, simply spending time with Jeff made me happy.

Shortly after that weekend, Jeff and I talked about taking a trip together to talk politics, sports, and life. The trip was just an excuse to enjoy each other's company for a few days, as we had done periodically over the years. But my job got too hectic, or I was too distracted, or something. The idea dissipated and we didn't go. I couldn't know then that I would never see Jeff again, but God, I wish I had made the time to take that trip.

On the morning of my birthday, August 11, 2011, Nancy called me with the terrible news that Jeff had died the day before. All this time later, I'm still numb to that fact and can't believe Jeff is gone. To this day I get the urge to call him when my Indians beat his beloved Orioles, or when something crazy happens in politics, or when I simply need a friend.

After Albert Einstein published the theory of relativity, someone supposedly asked him to explain relativity in layperson's terms. Einstein apparently said something like, "The theory of relativity boils down to this: When someone is hitting you with a stick, a minute feels like a lifetime. But when you're with someone you love, a lifetime feels like a minute."

For those of us who knew and loved Jeff Greer, it felt like too short a minute at that.

All my everlasting love,

Dad

ON THE WAY TO OUR NEW LIFE IN THE UNITED STATES

# Nineteen: Our National Character

Dear Mackenzie,

What is it about presidential politics that brings out the worst in America and Americans?

On the evening of May 8, 1964, that question was about the furthest thing from my seven-year-old mind. After bidding farewell to family and friends at the airport in Montevideo, Uruguay, your grandma and grandpa and your aunt Viv and I walked out onto a small, windy tarmac and boarded a Pan Am propeller plane to São Paulo, Brazil, where we'd connect to the much larger jet that would take us to our new life in the United States of America. I can't wait to show you pictures from that night. They look a bit like stills from the movie *Casablanca*.

It's hard to remember exactly how I felt at that moment. From the expression on my face in some of the pictures, it appears that I was pretty scared and that even at age seven I probably understood that we were heading toward an uncertain future. I do know that, like many immigrants before us, we held the belief that our destination was great and that opportunity would abound once we got there.

Over the years I've never stopped believing in the greatness of our country or in the American Dream. As a nation we have consistently shown the depth of our national character. From fighting the Nazis in World War II, to striving in the Civil Rights Movement, to ushering in the information age, we have repeatedly risen to the challenge and have sacrificed, in sweat and blood, so that future generations could have a better life. Except during the presidential election cycle. Then all hell breaks loose.

The 2008 presidential election was a great example. Over the course of the campaign, I watched with amused horror as one presidential hopeful after another said and did things on the national stage that made me fearful for the future of this country.

By way of background, for example, it has been well documented that while then congressman Newt Gingrich was ranting about family values and leading the charge to impeach President Clinton for the Paula Jones affair, he himself was cheating on his first wife, ultimately asking her for a divorce while she lay in a hospital fighting cancer.

The scoundrel mistress of his first marriage became the victim spouse of his second marriage when Gingrich cheated on her with a staffer twenty-five years his junior. I'm not suggesting that Gingrich has cheated on his current wife. I'm just saying that if I were her, I might keep a private investigator on retainer and a packed travel bag nearby.

When the press brought up all this information as he began his most recent run for the presidency, Gingrich responded that his infidelities had been partially caused by "how passionately I felt about this country." I guess he was trying to manifest that passion one constituent at a time. He also scolded the press, saying that to bring up these issues in a presidential campaign was "close to despicable."

During Michelle Bachmann's 2008 presidential run, the Minnesota congresswoman claimed that while slavery was not "perfect," African Americans may well have been better off as slaves because "at least their children got to grow up in two-parent households." I imagine it wasn't always clear who the two parents were, because history records that, among other things, the slave masters would rape their slaves with some regularity.

Rick Santorum, an ex-senator from Pennsylvania, gained momentum in his presidential bid by asserting that "having homosexual sex was one step above having sex with a dog or other animal." For good measure, he added that "the emotions of female soldiers would compromise the fulfilling of their combat duty."

These and other similar statements by presidential candidates are so patently absurd that it's hard to fathom that intelligent people like Gingrich, Bachmann, and Santorum actually believed what they were saying. It seems far more likely that these insidious statements were epithets designed to incite racist, homophobic, and misogynistic feelings in their core constituency. But even if these statements were more about pandering than genuine beliefs…really?

It's not an issue of left versus right. I have plenty of friends on both sides of the political aisle who speak eloquently on why they believe they're correct on the issues. If they can articulate a vision without resorting to cynicism and hate-mongering, why can't the candidates who aspire to the highest office in the land?

As things turned out, the campaign rhetoric in the 2008 presidential election paled in comparison to the 2016 election rhetoric. Worse, to a degree not seen in decades, the Trump presidency is causing actual and overt division and hatred among our citizenry long after the election cycle has ended. This new phenomenon worries me, my sweet daughter. Are the heart and soul of our national character disintegrating? Can it be that freedom of the press is truly in jeopardy? Do we really no longer believe that it's in every American's best interest to work for the collective good? We have never been at a more critical juncture in our nation's history. Yet at the very moment when we most need a true leader, we can't seem to find one. How do so many of us not care that our education and health care systems are in shambles, or that the middle class is in danger of extinction? I shudder at these thoughts.

We live in a world of sound bites, especially in politics. Yet when Ronald Reagan told us it was "morning in America," we got ready to face a new day. When Bill Clinton told us, "There is nothing wrong with this country that cannot be fixed by what is right with this country," we rolled up our sleeves and set about doing the hard work of repair. When Barack Obama told us, "Yes we can," we believed that yes we could.

No doubt those sound bites were written by speechwriters and marketing gurus, but at least those sound bites, and the people who used them, fed our positive national ethos. For me, at least, those statements resonate with my long-standing and unshakable belief that in these United States of America, a young immigrant boy from Montevideo, Uruguay, can still realize the American Dream, and achieve just about anything he sets his mind to if he's willing to work hard to do it.

The future lies in your hands, Mackenzie, and in the hands of other young people. Having been born in the USA, you won't feel the immigrant experience firsthand, as I did, but I hope you never take the principles of our great nation for granted, and that you'll fight to restore them to their past glory for future generations.

Even as I write you this letter, some family is boarding a plane in a faraway land on their way to a new life in the land of the free and the home of the brave—a journey not dissimilar to the one our family took some fifty years ago.

We can't let them down.

All my everlasting love,

Dad

# Twenty: Murder in the Family

Dear Mackenzie,

For the past several years you and I have had an ongoing daily patter that goes something like this:

Me: Do you know how much I love you?

You: Yes (or, channeling Buzz Lightyear: To infinity and beyond!).

Me: Do you know what I love best about you?

You: Everything.

Me: Will you remember forever?

You: Yes.

Me: You're such a winner.

The exchange always brings a smile to my face. To my great delight, our banter brings a smile to your face too. The back-and-forth has become a wonderful intimacy between us that I hope will continue forever. Not long ago someone overheard our little routine, and asked me how we came to start it.

One day a couple of years ago, I read an interview with a woman who had just been released from prison after serving eighteen years for killing her father. Needless to say, I was curious as to what had happened and why. The interview unsettled me, and I found myself googling similar stories.

I learned that without exception, every woman who had killed her father under similar circumstances had been the victim of repeated sexual, physical, or mental abuse—or all of the above, at the hands of the one man in the world who was charged by the forces of nature to protect her as she grew up. I was horrified. As the father of three daughters, and, frankly, as a human being, I found it shocking that a man could treat any girl or woman that way, let alone his own daughter.

I innately feel an overwhelming protective instinct toward you and your sisters, and I wondered what kind of man would drive his daughter to the point where she felt her only remaining choice was to defend herself by becoming a killer. More important, I worried about how to ensure that you would grow up feeling loved and respected in the way that you should as you make your way in the world.

I'm not a psychologist, and I leave the scientific analysis to those who are far more qualified than I am. But as a matter of common sense, it has always struck me that the best way to impart to you a sense of your self-worth, a sense of your "lump of clay" value, and a sense of your lovability is for your mom and me to manifest our love for you in tangible ways no matter what. And, as important, to tell you early and often (with apologies to Chicago politics) that whether we're angry with you or happy with you at any given moment, your mom and I love you unconditionally and forever.

I'm not saying I don't get angry with you or your sisters. Of course I do. A friend of mine once posted on Facebook that when she was a kid, sometimes her mom and dad would threaten to "knock her into the middle of next week" if she didn't start behaving. I had to laugh when I read that because every once in a while you do or say something that will cause me to understand that emotion. Yet I still want you to know that I love you even when you're driving me crazy.

When I was a teenager, your grandma would sometimes say to me, "If you love me, you'll clean your room." That always irritated me. How was one tied to the other? She could certainly ask me to clean my room, and she did. She could be upset with me if I then didn't clean my room, and she often was. But what did cleaning my room have to do with loving my mother?

And did that mean that if I didn't clean my room, I didn't love her? I certainly don't doubt that your grandma loved me, of course. Yet in adulthood I've come to understand that words are powerful tools. It's often easy for a parent to lose sight of the devastating impact words can have. The difference between innocuous venting and something much more nefarious isn't always distinguishable to a child's psyche.

Your mom and I know that for better or worse, we will be the most influential role models of your childhood. You'll be inclined to take our words and actions as gospel whether or not they are well intentioned.

As an athlete during my high school and college days, I had a few bad coaches and a few excellent coaches. The excellent ones taught me the importance of positive self-talk. They taught me that positive reinforcement and encouragement led to the self-talk of a winner. The bad ones? Well, enough said.

In the end, my sweet daughter, how you perceive yourself will become how other people perceive you too.

I've spent many years on the battlefield of life, and I know full well that the more one feels loved and lovable, the better one functions top to bottom. Experience has taught me the importance of love, and of respect, and of compassion. And, most important, experience has taught me the value of telling the people I love how much I actually love them. Which brings me back to how and why I started our little routine, and how I hope you'll go through life.

I wanted you to know you are profoundly loved, so that you may love others profoundly.

I wanted you to know you are unconditionally loved, so that you may love others unconditionally.

I wanted you to remember our love long after your mom and I are gone, so that you may pass that love on to your own children.

And I wanted you to know that you are a winner. Simply because you are.

Don't kill me for saying that.


All my everlasting love,


Dad

# Twenty-One: Listening

Dear Mackenzie,

Listen up.

I'm about to give you what may well be the best practical advice you'll ever get.

I'm not suggesting that you can't or won't succeed if you don't follow it. I am suggesting that if you follow what I'm about to tell you to the letter, you will be simply amazed by how people will flock to you in business and in life. I learned this lesson myself quite by accident, and it has made me a better husband, a better father, a better friend, and a better business executive.

If negotiating for a living has taught me anything at all, it's that most people don't listen during a conversation. It's not that people are rude or disinterested by nature. It's rather that most people are scared, and insecure, and a little self-obsessed.

I'll give you a few examples just to set the table.

I don't know if you've ever noticed, but most people are terrible with names. I'm convinced this is because when two people are introduced to each other, subconsciously each is more likely to listen for his or her own name than the name of the other person. The reason why two seconds later most people can't remember the other person's name is that they never actually hear it in the first place.

Here's another one. The last time you got in fight with a friend or a loved one, were you really listening while he or she told you what was causing the anger and hurt? Or were you using the time that the other person was talking to formulate in your own head what you were going to say next?

Active listening is the great competitive advantage in life, my sweet daughter. Very few people actually do it, especially in stressful situations. If you can actively listen to what someone is saying to you when the chips are down, you'll be way ahead of the game. It allows you to stay in the moment and to use real-time information in every context.

People are desperate to be heard. It's hardwired into the human condition. I have found that outside of politics, people usually don't even care whether you agree with them. What they do care about is whether you hear and really understand what they are trying to communicate to you.

Many, many years ago I attended a weekend therapy seminar with a very pretty friend. I grudgingly admit that I was far less interested in growing as a human being than I was in spending time with this particular person. Yet despite my selfish intentions, the weekend changed my life forever.

At some point during the seminar, the moderator had us all do a mirroring exercise. Everyone was paired up and told to role-play the thing they most wanted to say to someone who had injured them emotionally. So for example, I could pretend to talk to an old girlfriend. If I said, "Sally, you hurt me when you told me we could never have a future together and you didn't care," the person with whom I was partnered for the exercise would pretend to be Sally and would say, "What I hear you saying is…" and then mirror my sentence exactly. If they got it even slightly wrong, I would restate what I'd just said until the person could mirror it verbatim.

Once it was established that my words and feelings had been perfectly mirrored, the other person would say, "That makes all the sense in the world to me," followed immediately by, "If I were in your situation, I might feel the same way." That's it. Not a single variation.

Under the watchful eye of the moderator, the exercise went on for the better part of an afternoon. People were crying, laughing, yelling, and hugging as the cathartic exercise played out over and over. It was as if these were the most profound words anyone had ever spoken. I couldn't believe it.

Now at the time I was a brash, arrogant young guy who thought he knew everything. So at the break, I went up to the moderator and told him that with all due respect, the exercise was bogus. I explained that while rote regurgitation of another's words might work in an artificial therapy environment like this one, it would never work in the real world.

No doubt the moderator had been challenged like this in the past, because he smiled benignly and then suggested that for the next thirty days I use the technique in my business and personal life exactly as we had done it that day. He said if I didn't get results to my complete satisfaction, he would refund my money, no questions asked. Who could pass up an offer like that?

The first few times I tried it, I was awkward and embarrassed, certain that someone would call me on my "bullshit," or ask me if I was on drugs, or worse. And yet to my utter amazement, the more I mirrored what people were saying to me, and the more I acknowledged that what they were saying made sense to me, and the more I suggested that in their position I might feel the same way, the more I got the results I wanted personally and professionally. I became the beneficiary of my active listening, and I was giddy with delight. It was like a parlor trick.

Needless to say, I never called for a refund, and I've never looked back. The funny part, Mackenzie, is that if you do this consistently over time, you'll learn that active listening isn't a parlor trick at all. It's wonderfully real. Actually listening to people will deepen your enjoyment and appreciation of them. The more you listen to people and mirror them, the more genuinely interested you'll be in them. And they in you.

Imagine that.


All my everlasting love,


Dad

# Twenty-Two:
# The Arc of the Moral Universe

Dear Mackenzie,

On March 25, 1965, on the steps of the state capitol in Montgomery, Alabama, Martin Luther King Jr. delivered his famous "How Long, Not Long" speech, during which he said, "The arc of the moral universe is long, but it bends towards justice."

I have always loved that sentiment. I believe fervently in its truth and have relied on it during difficult times, even when the length of the arc has seemed excruciating. I hope you will abide by that sentiment in your own life, Mackenzie, and that you'll do your part to point the moral universe in the right direction. But how does that work as a practical matter?

When I lecture at colleges and universities around the country, I often talk about the "rule of 200." Basically the rule of 200 is that each of us knows about 200 people with whom we interact on some regular basis. If I do something very nice for you or otherwise help you in some way, you're likely to tell ten or twenty of those 200 people what a good person I am. But if I do something to harm you or to prejudice you in some way, you'll tell all 200 people what a bad person I am, and then go make new friends so you can bad-mouth me to them too.

Many years ago when I was practicing law, I found myself on the other side of a negotiation from a very inexperienced young attorney (we'll call him Dick—not his real name). Dick was cocky to the point of arrogance and even a little bit rude, yet as we continued to negotiate it became clear to me that he was in way over his head.

I got him to agree to a deal term so advantageous to my client, and so patently disadvantageous to his, that in my heart I knew the right thing would have been to point out his glaring error and teach him the issue for the future. But I didn't like Dick's attitude, and moreover, I wanted to play the hero. So instead, I called my client and told her what I had accomplished. The client was shocked and delighted.

The following morning I got a frantic call from Dick and his boss. Dick was chastened as his boss explained to me very respectfully that their client was furious and was threatening to fire their law firm. I knew I had taken advantage of Dick's inexperience, and Dick's boss was so classy I now felt bad. But since I had rushed to tell my client what a great job I'd done, I now had a problem of my own. Yet I also knew that unless I figured out how to give the other side some relief, the deal itself might be in jeopardy. And honestly, I didn't want Dick on my conscience either.

Long story short, I went back to my client hat in hand and disclosed what had happened. After plenty of grumbling, which could easily have been avoided had I done the right thing in the first place, my client relented. The matter now behind us, Dick called me and told me I had saved his job. He thanked me profusely, told me he would never forget my kindness, and promised that for the remainder of his career and mine I would have an endless supply of "get out of jail free" cards if ever I needed them. Fair enough.

Fade out, and then fade back in fifteen years later.

One day a young agent at my company came to see me in a panic. He explained that he had "screwed up royally" in a negotiation and that one of our clients was about to fire us because of his mistake. I had him explain the situation to me so I could help find a solution, and then asked who was on the other side of the deal.

You guessed it. It was Dick, who by now had become a successful entertainment attorney. I assured my young colleague that this would all work out fine and suggested we call Dick together. After some small talk, I humbly acknowledged to Dick that my young colleague had made a material mistake in the deal, and that we were now in grave jeopardy with our client.

To my utter amazement, Dick wouldn't budge. He told us that a deal's a deal and that our internal client management issue was not his problem. I was horrified. When we had called Dick, I'd had no intention of referencing what had happened those many years ago. I simply assumed that the universe was in alignment, and that I'd call in my chit with neither Dick nor me ever mentioning the past. But nothing we said moved him, even when I pointedly suggested that I would consider his help a personal favor to an old friend "from our early law days together."

Finally, I asked my young colleague to leave the room for a minute, and then told Dick that if he couldn't find it in his heart to help us for the right reasons, he should at least honor the promise he'd made to me fifteen years earlier when I'd stepped up to save his job. He refused, and indeed we ended up losing the client.

Will Dick ever get his comeuppance? I don't know. I tell this story quite often in my lectures, my sweet daughter, and I admit I've never found a truly satisfying answer to what its lesson should be.

That evil triumphs over good? That can't be it. That good triumphs over evil? That doesn't seem to fit either. Maybe the real lesson here is that it's not for us to keep the tally. Maybe how or when the arc of the moral universe bends, or even in which direction, shouldn't be what guides our own moral compass. Maybe our moral energy is best spent on how we conduct ourselves.

And let the universe worry about this Dick or that one.

All my everlasting love,

Dad

# Twenty-Three:
# How a Spider Saved My Life

Dear Mackenzie,

I've heard it said many times that the best way for people to understand the depth of their parents' love for them is to have children of their own. That's most certainly true. The prism through which you will view your mom and me as part of your childhood, Mackenzie, will be reflected in a very different hue once you become a caregiver too.

What could be more fulfilling to a parent, for example, than showing their kids how much they love them by showering them with affection? The very thought of enveloping one's child with hugs and kisses is enough to make almost any parent feel warm and fuzzy. It doesn't get a lot better than that. In my experience, though, it doesn't always go both ways.

A case in point: I still remember how when I was growing up, your grandma would try to hug me or kiss me at the most inopportune moments. I hated it. As I got a little older, it didn't feel like quite such an imposition, unless someone happened to be around when she tried to do it. Then I would instantly shut down your grandma's public display of affection. "Stop that, Mom," I would whine. "What are you doing?" Your grandma is no longer with us, of course, and what I wouldn't give today to get a hug or a kiss from her—publicly or otherwise.

Which brings me to you.

As you approach your teenage years, and given how willful and fiercely independent you are to begin with, I'm bracing myself for what my own parents and countless others have experienced through the ages. Hugs and kisses will hereafter be only grudgingly tolerated. Eye-rolling will become more frequent and dramatic when I try. You're going to be increasingly embarrassed by my stupid jokes (okay, fine, the whole family gets embarrassed by my stupid jokes, but you know what I mean). It has already started.

Many years from now, you may have a daughter of your own. Every so often she may push you away if you try to give her a hug. Every so often she may tell you that she hates you, which, depending on her age, could mean anything from "I'm unhappy you're not letting me eat a third cookie" to "I'm scared of the big, bad world out there but don't know how to tell you." Every so often she may even pretend not to know you when you pick her up from dance class, or she may demand that you don't get out of the car.

Cognitively you'll know she doesn't mean any harm by it. You'll remind yourself that like all normal, healthy young people, she's trying out different personas and reacting to the world around her. But it will still sting.

When that happens and you're at the end of your rope, my sweet daughter, don't hesitate to call your mom and me. We'll happily talk you through it if we're still reasonably lucid. First we'll instruct you to pour yourself a nice big glass of wine. That's very helpful in these situations. Then we'll remind you that parenting is not easy, and smile to ourselves at the notion that revenge is a dish best served cold.

Then a second glass of wine, this one for me, and I'll tell you about the time when you were about nine or ten and I was so overflowing with love for you that I came up behind you and surprised you with a great big hug and kiss. You jumped off the couch as if I'd just stabbed you with a saber, and started to yell at me. In that moment I wasn't self-possessed enough to process that your reaction had simply hurt my feelings. Instead I started yelling back at you and told you to go to your room until you were ready to apologize.

You flew up the stairs crying that you hated me. The whole exchange took less than thirty seconds, but it shook me to my core. How did an action emanating from such a feeling of love cause that horrible exchange? I sat in shock for about ten minutes, literally unable to move.

Suddenly you screamed, "Daddy!" at the top of your lungs with a tone of pure terror. I sprinted up the steps as you came running out of your bedroom. "What's wrong?" I asked, now in full protective mode. You responded that there was a really big spider in your room.

Your expression was a combination of fear about the spider and relief that I was there to handle it. I marched into your room to assert my dominance over the offending arachnid, and when the coast was clear you jumped into my arms with an "I love you, Daddy." The exchange of a few minutes before now seemed like ancient history. As my spirits soared, I said a silent prayer of thanks that God had seen fit to put that spider there, and that everything was once again right with the world. Well, maybe not for the spider.

The dynamics between parents and their children are complicated. It's the way of the world. That's the bad news, but it's the good news too.

To this day, I sometimes feel bad when I think about moments in my childhood when I didn't treat your grandparents as well as I should have, especially if it was in response to their showing me love. But now that I have daughters of my own, I know firsthand, as you will one day, that parents don't hold on to "I hate you." They treasure "I love you, Daddy" instead. And that's a wonderful thing both for parents and for their children.

Drink your wine, take a deep breath, and tell your daughter you love her.

All my everlasting love,

Dad

# Twenty-Four: Becoming Mia Hamm

Dear Mackenzie,

A couple of years ago you decided you wanted to play soccer. So your mom and I registered you with the local AYSO, and you were assigned to a team. I remember how excited you were when you got your uniform, how you wore it around the house for days, and how you said you couldn't wait for your first practice.

As we drove to the field, my sweet daughter, I started fantasizing about your potential future in soccer and what all that could mean for you. I also started reminiscing about the not-so-distant past.

On a blistering hot day in July of 1999, three friends and I drove to the Rose Bowl in Pasadena, California, along with 90,000 other people, to watch the finals of the Women's World Cup. I'd never been much of a soccer fan, let alone of the women's game. Yet along with much of the rest of the nation, I'd been riveted as the U.S. team defeated Germany, and then mighty Brazil, to advance to the finals. Mia Hamm, Julie Foudy, Kristine Lilly, and others had captured our imaginations and we wanted to experience them, and the moment, firsthand.

By any objective measure, the game turned out to be as incredible a sporting event as I'd ever attended. Both teams fought valiantly. Many spectators wilted in the sweltering heat, and it would have been completely understandable if the players had too. Yet neither side did. Regulation time ended with the teams in a scoreless tie, as did the overtime period.

The fans roared throughout the entire penalty shootout as each side took its respective turns. When Briana Scurry made a diving save of a kick from one of the Chinese players, it felt as if we were in the midst of an earthquake. The very foundation of the stadium was rocked by the foot-stomping and by the sound of 90,000 people chanting, "USA! USA!"

And then Brandi Chastain made the final kick of the shootout, and the 99ers became World Cup champions. The feeling inside the stadium in that moment, and no doubt in front of millions of television sets across the country, was one of unparalleled catharsis and jubilation.

Chastain famously took off her T-shirt and whirled it around as she sank to her knees, and not a single fan left the stadium for a good hour or more after the game. Players hugged each other. Fans hugged each other. Players hugged fans. Fans hugged players. A lifetime's worth of exaltation and celebration played out in front of me.

Many of the life lessons that sports teach us, as well as the traits one needs to become a champion, had been in full evidence throughout the match. Teamwork. Dedication. Courage. Perseverance. Resilience. Hard work. The thrill of victory. And, unfortunately for the Chinese team, the agony of defeat too.

What Brandi, Mia, and the gang left on the field that day, and how they did it, shaped Hope Solo and Alex Morgan's generation, is shaping your generation, and will shape all future generations who follow. The 99ers showed millions of young people, and especially young girls, that you can achieve anything you set your mind to and are willing to work for. These players also taught us that grace, power, athleticism, and beauty are not mutually exclusive, and that champions come in all shapes, colors, sizes, and yes, genders.

As befits a doting dad, I thought how great it would be if one day you were able to experience a similar life-affirming sporting event. Maybe you'd watch Hope Solo make a gamewinning save at goal during the finals of the 2015 World Cup. Maybe you'd watch Sydney Leroux bury one from the corner to help the USA win the 2019 World Cup.

I even wondered privately if you yourself might one day become a Mia Hamm or an Alex Morgan. Maybe in the final seconds of the 2023 Women's World Cup finals, a young rookie on the national team named Mackenzie Aladjem would pass the ball from the right wing with surgical accuracy to a grizzly veteran named Megan Rapinoe coming across the middle, who in turn would score the winning goal as time ran out and a delirious crowd yelled, "*Goooooooaaaaaaaa/////////!!!*"

These were the thoughts that raced through my mind as we pulled up to the park. You were nervous, and since you didn't know any of the girls on the team, your mom walked you over to the coach. We watched you run around during practice, and you seemed to be having loads of fun. At one point someone passed you the ball and you took a shot on goal. Though the kick went wide of the mark, you were grinning from ear to ear. If I didn't know better, I would have sworn you were posing at the point of impact instead of focusing on the ball, but I was delighted nonetheless.

Team pictures were taken at the second practice, and I think you were more excited about that than about the practice itself. When the proofs came, you picked several of the shots for us to print, and then happily announced you didn't want to play anymore. Just like that, your soccer career was over.

Periodically you ask me to take you to the park and we kick the ball around, but at least so far that seems to be the extent of your interest in the sport. Unless you change your mind, it looks like the 2023 national team will have to win without you.

A sports trophy is certainly a wonderful, tangible reminder of one's achievement. Yet that's not the complete story of a champion. Mia Hamm was only thirty-two years old when she retired, a full life and another career (or more) still ahead of her. During the first half of her final game, Mia wore her normal jersey, with her usual number nine under the name Hamm. When she came out of the tunnel to start the second half, though, she was wearing a jersey with the name Garciaparra over her number instead, a tip of the hat to the new adventures that lay ahead of her.

Since her retirement, Mia has become a co-owner of Los Angeles FC, a professional soccer team; is a global ambassador for FC Barcelona; wrote a book called *Go for the Goal: A Champion's Guide to Winning in Soccer and in Life*; and has been featured in several films and television shows. How's that for a second act? And she's married with three children to boot.

The lessons Mia learned with the 99ers will stay with her forever. I hope those lessons will also shine their light on you, and that you'll be a champion in life, whether or not you ever kick another soccer ball.

By the way, I still have the cutest picture ever of you in your soccer uniform. I may even take it with me to the games in 2023.

All my everlasting love,

Dad

# Twenty-Five: Playing God

Dear Mackenzie,

Everybody likes to play God now and again. It feels like it would be great fun to make life-or-death decisions. But in the real world, those decisions have consequences.

Many years ago I had a wonderful golden retriever named Banana. She was my loyal companion for more than thirteen years, until her death in 2000. I still miss her a lot.

When Banana got sick, the vet told me that there was a small chance that surgery might extend her life. Of course I wanted that if at all possible. But at the same time, I didn't want her last days to be spent in an animal hospital hooked up to machines.

After consulting with several veterinary surgeons and doing much soul-searching, I decided we had to try. So Banana went under the knife. The surgeon called me after the surgery and told me the operation had been successful. She predicted Banana and I could look forward to some additional quality time together in the future. The surgeon said I could come see Banana the following day, and that with any luck she would be home within the week. I was beyond relieved.

Early the next morning, however, the surgeon called again to say there had been a major complication. She explained that unless she operated again immediately, Banana would not survive the day. A number of hours later I was told that Banana was again out of surgery and that I should come visit her. But before I got there, Banana died.

Hindsight is 20/20. Yet every once in a while I'm still tortured about my decision. Had I been selfish to have her undergo surgery? Should I have let her wonderful life end on a much more graceful note? Had I played God for her sake or mine?

Life went on, and when you were about a year old, we got another golden retriever, which Jamie named Dixie. Time went by.

Then in late October of 2010, Heather noticed that Dixie was getting increasingly lethargic. We monitored her for a few days, and when she didn't seem to be getting any better, Jamie and I decided to take her to the vet as a precaution. You and Mom were living in New York at the time, since you were working on *Nurse Jackie*, but Dixie was only eight, so no one was overly concerned.

The vet examined Dixie thoroughly and told us she had very advanced cancer and had only days to live. She said there was nothing that could be done for her, and sympathetically suggested that though the choice was ours, it might be best for Dixie if we euthanized her right then and there.

Only days to live? Euthanize her that day? What was she talking about? We were numb.

I called my friend Nancy who is very involved with dog rescue and knows the best vets around Los Angeles. Nancy referred me to a specialist, who in turn referred us to another specialist, but everyone said the same thing. Dixie couldn't be saved, and a natural death from what Dixie had would be a painful one. We were fighting both the clock and Mother Nature.

With very heavy hearts, on the evening of November 1, 2010, Heather, Jamie, and I took Dixie on her last car ride. Late that night, I sat in bed and wrote your mom the following email:

*Hi Honey,*

*I didn't want to call you because it's almost 3 AM in New York and hopefully you and Mackie are asleep.*

*Dixie went to her play date with Banana about 10 PM tonight. She seemed calm and peaceful and not at all afraid. They laid down a blanket for her in a room and Dixie lay on it wagging her tail and happy. Heather, Jamie, and I petted her and held her and kissed her until the end.*

*Dixie had a wonderful last couple of days. I sense that she was happy that Heather was there, and she was showered with love from all sides. Five or six of Jamie's friends threw Dixie a goodbye brunch yesterday and she was the center of attention, which she loved. I think the only thing Dixie would have loved more would have been if you and*

Mackenzie could have been there as well. At least she got to Skype with you both. Wait till she tells her friends in doggie heaven that she was Skyping! Today she ate McDonald's, matzo ball soup, pepperoni, and countless dog biscuits. She was a happy girl.

You should know that Heather and Jamie were beyond courageous. I know how hard it was for me to be in the room at the end, so I can only imagine what it was like for them. But they never faltered, not for an instant. You would have been so proud of them. I sure was. You have raised two wonderful, amazing young women and it is such a gift that I get to be part of their lives. Heather of course wears her heart on her sleeve and Jamie, for all of her gruff exterior, is remarkably profound.

The one other thing that bears saying is how proud and amazed I am by how Mackenzie handled all of this. I was just rereading some of her Facebook posts and it's incredible how resilient, profound, kind, loving, and wise she is for a nine-year-old.

As you said, Dixie left us too soon. She was never the most easygoing dog in the world. She was not the best-trained dog. Given her temperament, she may have been better served being an only dog. And I have sometimes wondered if given our crazy lives over the past few years, we didn't make a mistake not giving her to Jenny Lee at that time.

But all in all Dixie was a happy dog, and she had a wonderful life. She was more bonded to you than anyone (don't tell Heather I said that) and you rewarded her love, as you do to all whom you touch, by loving her unconditionally, and caring for her, and making her feel the gift of you in a hundred ways every day you were together.

I love you more than I can say, and I wish you were here to comfort all of us as only you can.

xoxo Norm

As it turns out, my sweet daughter, playing God is not all it's cracked up to be.

All my everlasting love,

Dad

# Twenty-Six: Immortality

Dear Mackenzie,

Woody Allen once wrote: "Most people want to achieve immortality through their work. I want to achieve it by not dying." Unfortunately, not dying is not an option. So in that case, what does "immortality" really mean?

A few weeks ago I thought you told me you were going to organize a lemonade stand with Alex. I acknowledge that I was not listening as actively as I should have been (the Dodgers were on television). I remember thinking at the time that I wasn't sure who Alex was, but that putting a lemonade stand together sounded like a fun, entrepreneurial play date.

Subsequently your mom posted about it on Facebook, and I realized that what you were actually planning was to raise money for a charity called Alex's Lemonade Stand Foundation (ALSF), which benefits childhood cancer research. I saw in Mom's post that you were doing this in memory of your late uncle Reed, who had himself died of childhood leukemia. I was proud and impressed.

Then about a week ago, you and Mom started preparing the lemonade stand, and my curiosity was piqued. What exactly was this foundation, and more important, who was Alex?

According to the ALSF website, Alexandra "Alex" Scott was born to Liz and Jay Scott in Manchester, Connecticut, on January 18, 1996, the second of four children.

The website goes on to say that shortly before her first birthday, Alex was diagnosed with neuroblastoma, a type of childhood cancer. On her first birthday, the doctors informed Alex's parents that even if she were able to beat her cancer, it was doubtful that Alex would ever walk again. The website further says that just two weeks later, Alex slightly moved her leg at her parents' request to kick, and that this was the first indication of who she would turn out to be: a determined, courageous, confident, and inspiring child with big dreams and big accomplishments.

Alex appeared to be beating the odds, until the shattering discovery within the next year that her tumors had started growing again. In the year 2000, the day after her fourth birthday, Alex received a stem cell transplant and informed her mother, "When I get out of the hospital, I want to have a lemonade stand." She said she wanted to give the money to doctors to allow them to "help other kids, like they helped me." True to her word, she held her first lemonade stand later that year with the help of her older brother and raised an amazing two thousand dollars for "her" hospital.

I also learned from the website that while bravely battling her own cancer, Alex and her family continued to hold yearly lemonade stands in their front yard to benefit childhood cancer research. The news spread of the remarkable sick child dedicated to helping other sick children. People from all over the world, moved by her story, set up their own lemonade stands and donated the proceeds to Alex and her cause.

Alex passed away in August of 2004 at the age of eight. By the time she died, Alex had helped raise more than a million dollars from around the world to help find a cure for childhood cancer. Since her death, Alex's family has been committed to continue Alex's inspiring legacy through the ALSF.

As I write you this letter, my sweet daughter, the ALSF has become a national fundraising movement, and ALSF has raised more than fifty million dollars, and counting, in Alex's memory to combat different childhood cancers. I hope you'll continue to read the ALSF website as time goes by to see what amazing things the foundation accomplishes.

On Sunday, June 10, 2012, a warm and beautiful day in Toluca Lake, you and your friend Camden set up the lemonade stand on the front lawn of our house. Your mom, Camden's mom, Jamie, Heather, and I savored your efforts and the magnificent morning as you and Camden hawked lemonade to fight cancer.

Friends and neighbors stopped by to help, and chatted while sipping lemonade and eating cookies. Our neighbor Steve gave a generous donation, and also donated some gourmet cookies to add to your sales inventory. Our friend Melissa stopped by with a generous donation, and also brought delicious homemade cupcakes for you to sell (I cannot tell a lie; I bought several). By 2 PM, between online donations and your and Camden's efforts on the front lines, you had raised more than twelve hundred dollars for the charity.

Of course it's wonderful that you raised a lot of money for cancer research. But what was really wonderful, what filled me with love and admiration for you and what you did, was how you and Camden brought Alex and her memory to life.

You told everyone who came by our house that day about Alex's life story, and about her courage, and about how she had started this amazing movement that is living on beyond her time on this earth. So in a way, you really did have a play date with Alex on Sunday.

From what I've read about Alex's life and her courage, I'm sorry I never had the opportunity to meet her. I'm not sure that I would have the resolve to accomplish what she did in her situation, let alone before the age of eight. And I wonder whether I would have the spiritual enlightenment to try to help others even as I was dying. Alex must have been a truly special kid.

I can tell you as a parent, Mackenzie, that Alex's family would trade all her accomplishments, and all the good that has come from her terrible situation, and all the tea in China, to have Alex still here with them. And given a choice, I suspect she might have too. That wasn't in the cards for Alex, though, who instead got something else entirely.

Immortality.

All my everlasting love,

Dad

# Twenty-Seven:
# The Wisdom of Mike Tyson

Dear Mackenzie,

No one ever accused former heavyweight boxing champ Mike Tyson of being quotable. Yet one of my all-time favorite quotes about life comes straight from the lips of the great pugilist. "Everyone has a plan," he once said, "until he gets punched in the mouth." Tyson was talking literally, of course. But his quote has universal applicability.

Not long ago I was involved in a difficult movie negotiation on behalf of a client. The producer took my side against the studio, and I was surprised not only by the fact that he jumped into the fray, but also by the skill and ferocity with which he fought. At lunch one day not long afterward, I thanked him for his help and told him I had been impressed by how he had handled himself. He told me he had gotten involved because he had been offended by the studio's position. "I don't like to fight," he said, "but I know how to do it."

But shouldn't we avoid fighting?

Not always. I have learned in life that sometimes fighting, or at least being willing to fight, serves a very useful purpose. I took an anthropology class in college. I learned that throughout history, when a warring tribe encountered a peaceful tribe and each tribe interacted with the other in a manner consistent with its nature, without exception the warring tribe annihilated the peaceful tribe.

I learned this lesson myself the hard way, my sweet daughter. When we moved to the United States, my parents enrolled your aunt Viv and me in the local elementary school, and I entered the third grade. At the time I didn't speak English, and more to the point I was small for my age. In the time-honored *Lord of the Flies* tradition, other boys started picking on me.

I pretended not to notice, or pretended that it didn't bother me. I could outrun just about everyone in my class if need be anyway. What I couldn't outrun was the alienation and low self-esteem I felt. I was afraid to tell your grandma and grandpa what was going on, because I thought they would step in and talk to the teachers or the principal. I feared that would only make things worse.

In sixth grade our family moved from Cleveland, Ohio, to Augusta, Georgia, and I enrolled in a new school. By then I was fluent in the language, but I was still the new kid, and still pint-sized. To make things worse, at that age boys' testosterone starts to kick in, causing them to start noticing girls and to look for ways to impress them. The bigger boys started picking on me again.

Brenda Nance changed my life forever. Brenda was this beautiful, auburn-haired girl in my class with sparkling eyes and the cutest freckles you ever saw. She didn't know it then, and she likely has no recollection of who I am, but in the sixth grade I had a huge crush on her. I wasn't the only boy in the class who did.

One morning in the school hallway, a large kid tried to pick a fight with me and started calling me names. I almost certainly would have ignored him had Brenda not been standing right there. I was petrified, but no way was I going to let her think I was a wimp. So I told the bully that he should "meet me after school."

"Meet me after school" was a popular and ongoing event in sixth grade. Since you couldn't fight during school without getting in trouble, disputes were settled in the playground after school was out. All the kids would come and cheer for whichever fighter was their friend. No one got badly hurt, and the fights didn't last long, because no one wanted to miss the school bus and have to explain why to his parents.

I spent the rest of that day in mortal fear. I couldn't eat. I couldn't study. I couldn't think of anything other than that I was going to get an ass-whooping. Yet at 3:10 PM that day, I arrived at the appointed place to meet my destiny. A dozen or more classmates were there to watch the new kid get beat up. I resisted the strong impulse to run.

The bully started to taunt and shove me, and then pushed me to the ground. To this day I remember vividly that out of the corner of my eye I saw the assistant principal heading toward us to break up the fight. All I had to do was stay down another thirty seconds and it would be over. But then I saw Brenda.

So instead I got up and lunged at the other kid with everything I had, somehow landing a couple of punches. In the movie version of my life story, Brenda will look at me with something resembling young love as I knock the other kid unconscious. In real life, the moment I landed my first punch, the other kid unleashed on me with a fury, and by the time the assistant principal broke it up, I had both a fat lip and the beginnings of a terrible black eye.

But I had something else too. I had the respect of my schoolmates, who saw my black eye as a badge of courage. Perhaps more important, I had my self-respect, which from that day forward I've never lost. These days, most people who know me would probably describe me as an easygoing, friendly sort. Yet people who have confused my affable nature with weakness have regretted it.

So when should you fight, Mackenzie? Believe it or not, you'll know instinctively. Don't go looking for fights, physical or otherwise. Walk away when you can. Give peace a chance.

If that doesn't work, listen to Mike Tyson.

All my everlasting love,

Dad

# Twenty-Eight: Love Gone Wrong

Dear Mackenzie,

Each week for the past six months, I've essentially written you a love letter. I pick a theme that I hope will interest you when you reach adulthood, and then I weave a narrative around it using your life experiences and mine. The letters are fun to write, hopefully inspiring, and fulfilling beyond measure.

On another side of town, several afternoons each month I write narratives of a different kind. These also weave a theme around life experiences, but they are not at all fun to write. They are not inspiring either, although in a different way I find fulfillment in writing them too.

Room 245 of the Los Angeles County Superior Court is a courtroom in the family law area of the downtown courthouse. A sign that reads "Temporary Restraining Orders" hangs ominously over the door. It's a daunting place. Every day at precisely 8:00 AM and 1:00 PM, a sheriff unlocks the doors and a long line of people make their way in, hoping to get urgent relief from a spouse or significant other who is beating them, threatening to inflict great bodily injury on them, or otherwise abusing them.

In the back of the courtroom sits a little bullpen area with run-down furniture and outdated computers. Three staffers from the LA County Domestic Violence Project and a rotating handful of volunteers listen to people's stories and help victims of domestic violence prepare forms and declarations to submit to a judge. The judge then decides on the spot whether or not to grant the restraining order based on the application.

On the second and fourth Tuesday of each month, I donate a little of my time and what's left of my legal brain in one of the volunteer cubicles. The stories we hear shouldn't shock me, but they consistently do. *Law & Order: SVU* has nothing on these real-life victims.

A very attractive and conservatively dressed young woman entered our bullpen one day looking like a deer in the headlights. She couldn't have been more that twenty-five years old, and she looked like she had gone ten rounds with Manny Pacquiao. Her blonde bangs partially hid two black eyes, and a deep bruise went all the way around her neck like a choker. Abrasions adorned her left shoulder like so many tattoos.

As we helped her prepare a declaration for the judge, I thought that there but for the grace of God went Heather, Jamie, or you. My heart ached for the young woman, and I wondered how I would react if someone violated one of you like that. I suspect it would take every fiber of my being to not track down the person who did it and beat him to a pulp myself. I reminded myself that for all its inefficiency, at least a legal venue exists where one can get help without taking the law into his or her own hands.

The stories of the people who come to the Domestic Violence Project are all different, but the narratives are the same. A guy repeatedly comes home drunk and beats his wife. A woman tells her boyfriend she is breaking up with him, so he threatens to kill her and their young son or daughter. A man thinks his fiancée is cheating on him, so he takes a baseball bat to her car and tells her she's next. A man abuses and humiliates his undocumented girlfriend, and tells her that if she speaks up he will have her deported and make sure she loses her child.

The large majority of domestic abuse victims are female, but they're not exclusively so. I wrote a declaration for a guy whose girlfriend put sugar in his gas tank and then tried to set him on fire. I wrote one for a guy whose ex would come to his workplace and threaten to kill him and everyone at the company.

It goes on and on until your head starts to spin and your stomach is in knots. By the way, my sweet daughter, the victims are not always sympathetic. The fiancée whose significant other thought she was cheating on him in fact was, and openly. She said she wanted to "humiliate him for having a menial job." The guy whose girlfriend threatened him and his coworkers had shown the coworkers pictures of her in compromising positions and then bragged to her about it.

The judicial system doesn't allow for personality, though. Unsympathetic people have the same rights as sympathetic ones. If you don't like that I'm cheating on you, you get to leave me or sue me for divorce. Yet the law is pretty clear that you don't get to physically assault me. If you think I'm not good enough for you, you get to try to improve your lot. You don't get to set me on fire, or threaten our children, or stalk me at work, or take a wrought iron pole to my head.

Why do people resort to domestic violence? Lots of reasons, it seems. They get angry. They get frustrated. They feel impotent. They don't feel heard. They feel humiliated. They perceive that they have no options. The crazy part is that their feelings are often valid. It's an unavoidable fact of life that people are sometimes unkind to each other. That's a difficult pill to swallow. Yet justified or not, these feelings don't give us the right to beat each other up.

Unfortunately, leaving is also easier said than done, and doubly so if you're indigent, or undocumented, or don't speak the language, or don't even have a car in which to leave.

And so people go at each other instead, and I continue to go to the courthouse every couple of weeks and write declarations of pain to give to a judge.

I pray you and your sisters are never in need of these particular declarations. I'll be there for you if you do, of course, but I much prefer writing you my declarations of love.

All my everlasting love,

Dad

# Twenty-Nine: The Downside of Passion

Dear Mackenzie,

In a perfect world we'd all get everything we want, especially if we're willing to work for it. But that's not always how life works.

About two weeks ago you flew to NYC with Mom to audition for the lead in a Broadway musical called *Matilda*. The show is based on the 1996 film of the same name, directed by Danny DeVito. It's about a wonderful little girl (Matilda) who, along with her teacher, teams up against the worst parents imaginable and the worst principal imaginable.

The show was scheduled to move to Broadway, and auditions were being held for that production. You couldn't have been more excited when your agent called your mom to say the creative team wanted to see you for the role of Matilda.

I watched in silent amazement as you prepared for the audition. For weeks before you went to NYC, you took voice lessons specifically geared to Matilda, took dance classes geared to Matilda, worked on your sides, ran lines, and listened to the soundtrack religiously.

I wasn't really surprised. Despite your happy-go-lucky nature, for a person your age you seem unusually committed to your craft. That said, both your mom and I noticed that for this particular project your passion was palpable, and you ratcheted things up a notch or two. I didn't say anything to you or even to your mom, but as I dropped you guys off at the airport I had a sense you were going to get this role.

At the audition you were told that of all things, you might be too tall and mature for the role by the time the show opened. But the next day, Mom heard from your agent that they wanted to see you again for a callback. Apparently you were so happy and so relieved by that news that you sat down in the hotel room and cried for ten minutes.

Your mom told me I sounded very nonchalant when I spoke with you, and truth be told I felt it. I don't know why, but I was convinced you were going to be Matilda on Broadway. You went for a second callback, and then a third. And then your agent called Mom again. You weren't going any further. Everyone involved had said they loved your work and your passion for the role, but that you were definitely going to be too tall and mature for the role by the time the show opened the following year. They were going to look for someone younger.

You were inconsolable. Mom told me that in the years you'd been acting and auditioning, she had never seen you this upset about not getting a role. When you and I got on the phone, I tried to give you a pep talk and told you how proud I was of you, but you shut me down and refused to even talk about it. You were devastated.

As you might imagine, my sweet daughter, your upset has eaten away at me. Throughout your career (can a ten-year-old have a career?) I have been careful to always ask you a version of only one question: Were you having fun with that audition, or that part, or those lessons? I've assiduously stayed away from asking you how something went, or whether you did well, or whether the casting people liked you.

My hope has always been that framing the questions in that manner would diminish the competitive aspect of what you've chosen to do, and thus maximize your enjoyment. But now you're almost eleven, and your psyche is no longer oblivious to the pressure, or to the fact that you are competing for these roles at the highest level. Add to that the capricious nature of decisions about acting roles (you're too tall, you're too short, you're too blonde, you're not blonde enough, and so on) and the pressure cooker can no longer be ignored.

Like all parents, your mom and I suffer when we see you in distress. We want to protect you and your young heart in every way possible, and it pains us when we can't. The downside of being passionate about something you love is that you commit to it fully but you don't always succeed at it. If you give your blood, sweat, and tears to that thing and you still fall short, the pain and disappointment are that much more profound.

On the flight home, you were discouraged and distraught. You had come very close on three or four projects in the past month or so and hadn't booked any of them. You asked Mom why that was happening, but unfortunately there's no good answer to that question. Mom asked you if you were still enjoying the process and whether you wanted to continue or take a little time off to do other things. You were adamant that you wanted to continue.

You'll always have ups and downs in your career and in your life. Maybe you'll make it big as an artist and maybe you won't. I hope you do if it's what you want, but there are no guarantees.

So what's a parent to do? I'm not sure. In the end, I guess your mom and I will do what we've always done. We'll encourage you to do what you love. We'll make sure that if you're competing, it's because that's what you want to do, and not because it's what someone else thinks you should do. We'll celebrate with you in success, and we'll try to comfort you in failure. And mostly, we'll just root for you and love you and believe in you, however it all plays out.

That said, I admit that although I haven't seen the show, I think the Broadway production of *Matilda* would benefit from the lead character's being a little bit taller. I'm just sayin'.

All my everlasting love,

Dad

# Thirty: Helping People

Dear Mackenzie,

Sometimes the most innocent beings teach us the most enduring lessons.

One night a week or so ago, I was feeling quite sorry for myself. A particular person whom I have helped a lot over the years in his career had an opportunity to help me with a certain piece of business and didn't. It wasn't a big deal really, but I found out quite by accident and given my history with this person, I felt slighted.

I started complaining to your mom about the injustice of the universe. I wondered out loud why I had ever helped him in the first place. What was the point? What had I been thinking? Why help anyone?

You must know by now, Mackenzie, that your mom is much wiser and more centered than I am. And she usually sees right through my nonsense. As I continued to pout, she asked me why I had initially helped the person. Was it so that one day he could help me with something? If so, she said, then business is what business is. I had made a calculated decision about a person or his willingness to help me and had simply been wrong. It happens. She gently suggested that I should quit complaining and move on.

I argued that wasn't the case at all. I said I had helped him because I had seen something in him that made me believe he had been worthy of my help. Your mom countered that if that were true, then my satisfaction should come purely from the act of helping him, irrespective of whether he returned the favor. She again gently suggested that I should quit complaining and move on.

I didn't like her analysis one bit, by which I mean it didn't serve my pouting mood. I explained that in our society, helping people was a complex dynamic that couldn't and shouldn't be so easily categorized. I suggested that the issue wasn't nearly that black and white. Or some such psychobabble.

But I was losing steam, and the argument, and I knew it. So I retreated to my Google News to regroup. And there I read a humbling article about a nine-year-old girl named Anaiah Rucker.

On the morning of February 4, 2011, Anaiah and her five-year-old sister, Camry, left their house in Madison, Georgia, to go to school. According to news reports, their mother watched from the porch of the family home, as she did every day, when the girls started to cross the street to the school bus stop.

It was raining heavily, and both girls had on their hoodies to try to stay a little bit dry. Probably because of that, neither girl noticed the truck that was barreling toward them as they ran out onto the road. By the time Anaiah saw the truck it was too late. She realized that she and her little sister were about to be hit and that she had only an instant to jump backward out of harm's way.

Jumping out of harm's way is exactly what most of us would have done. Certainly no one would have questioned a nine-year-old girl's acting on the instinct of self-preservation. But Anaiah didn't do that. Instead, she did just the opposite. As her mother watched in horror from the house, Anaiah jumped in front of her little sister and pulled Camry backward to safety, absorbing the brunt of the impact herself.

Anaiah collapsed on the ground, all but dead. She stopped breathing, and her heart stopped. The driver of the school bus, Lorretta Berryman, who was approaching the stop as the terrible event unfolded, ran to her side and performed CPR until paramedics arrived on the scene and rushed her to the hospital.

Both of Anaiah's legs were fractured, her neck was broken, her spleen and a kidney were damaged, and who knows what else. For ten desperate hours, doctors worked to save Anaiah's life. They amputated her leg, removed her kidney, reset her fractured neck, and otherwise fought to put Humpty Dumpty back together again. Five surgeries and six weeks later, Anaiah came home from the hospital.

As you might imagine, my sweet daughter, the story made national news. Once she could talk again (apparently she could communicate only by blinking her eyes for the first month or so after the accident), the media barraged Anaiah with questions about her heroics. What had gone through her mind in that moment? Why had she done what she'd done? On *The Today Show*, the courageous nine-year-old answered simply that she had wanted to help her little sister. Her agenda was straightforward and pure.

Compared to Anaiah's actions, I felt like a bit of an idiot for worrying about what someone "had done for me lately." And as usual, your mom was right (don't tell her I said that). Yet truth be told, the question continues to gnaw at me. What do we owe to those who help us along the way? I'm not sure.

In a perfect world, the friend I had helped would have directed the piece of business my way and there would have been balance in the universe. Okay, so he didn't. But does that make him a villain?

Maybe he simply didn't think of me in that moment. Maybe he felt that directing that particular business elsewhere was more beneficial to him than directing it toward me. Is that so wrong? What if he was actually trying to pay it forward? Doesn't he get to do that? I hate to admit it, but I think he does.

I guess in the end, you help people when you can and if at some point it comes back to you, that's gravy. I can live with that.

But as the trucks of life come barreling toward you at warp speed, Mackenzie, may the Anaiahs of the world be at your side.

All my everlasting love,

Dad

# Thirty-One: The Law of Attraction

Dear Mackenzie,

There's a scene in an old Chuck Norris movie from 1986 where Chuck Norris' character and his foil, played by Louis Gossett Jr., are stranded in a Mexican jungle. It's an action-adventure film, but at its core the movie is about two guys, one of whom (Norris) is an eternal optimist and one of whom (Gossett) is an eternal pessimist.

At one point Gossett turns to Norris and complains that they are lost. "We're not lost," says Norris. "We're just off-course."

"What's the difference?" asks Gossett.

"Attitude," replies Norris.

The other night I was sharing a taxi in NYC with our friends Lindsay and Devyn. We were discussing the letters I've been writing to you, and Devyn and Lindsay were giving me their thoughts about the impact these letters might have on you when you read them as an adult. They also commented on the impact the letters are having on them now as young women making their way in the world.

I was flattered by their kind words, and I decided to ask them if there was a particular topic they thought might be interesting or beneficial for a young person to ponder. Without hesitation, Lindsay suggested that I write about the law of attraction.

I assumed she was saying I should write you a letter about pheromones and what attracts people to each other, or about the things people do and say when they're in love, or about the notion that beauty is subjective ("in the eye of the beholder"), or maybe even about how a person's self-esteem is impacted by society and by Madison Avenue.

Those are all interesting issues, actually, and maybe I'll write to you about them sometime. As it turns out, though, Lindsay was referring to the belief that "like attracts like" and the notion that by focusing on positive thoughts or negative thoughts, one can actually bring about positive or negative results.

A well-documented example of the law of attraction is most commonly experienced in medical trials and is called the placebo effect. The placebo effect in clinical trials refers to the phenomenon that subjects who believe they will be positively affected by a certain medication fare better than those who do not, even when they are given a sugar pill instead of actual medication.

Similarly, the medical literature talks about the nocebo effect. In clinical trials, that's when a subject experiences negative side effects or other negative consequences due to a negative image of a certain medication. It has been documented that these negative results are very real even in instances when the subject is not given the medication at all but rather is given a sugar pill.

But can that really be? Is it possible that ultimately you can if you think you can, and you can't if you think you can't? Obviously it isn't that simple. There's a lot to be said for positive thinking, of course. Yet jumping off a tall building because you believe you can fly can get you killed, no matter how genuine your belief. And it doesn't matter how legitimately I think I'm better than LeBron James. He can take me to the hoop a hundred times out of a hundred.

And what about the converse? Can you find love if you don't think you're worthy of love? Can you solve a math problem if you don't think you're good at math? These are all fascinating questions.

I have a friend who keeps an aquarium filled with exotic fish. He prides himself on being able to keep predator fish in the same tank as other fish that would normally be their lunch. Here's what he does.

First, he puts all the fish in the same tank and separates them with a clear, hard plastic plate. When a predator fish tries to get to the other side to eat its quarry, it runs into the invisible wall and can't get past. After a week or so of doing this, the fish gives up because it no longer believes it can get to the other side. By the time my friend removes the clear plastic plate, the predator fish stays on its side of the tank on its own.

I have no idea if that consistently works (please, don't try this with fish you don't want to lose), but either way it makes the point. Your mind and your psyche are incredibly powerful instruments, Mackenzie. We will usually not achieve what we believe we can't achieve, because consciously or otherwise we will not try. If we don't believe we are worthy of love, we will sabotage efforts by others to love us. In very large measure, losers lose simply because they expect to.

On the other hand, winners expect to win. Positive thinking by itself is not enough, but it's the foundation of success. As the late noted motivational speaker Zig Ziglar used to say, positive thinking will let you do everything better than negative thinking will.

As you go through life, my sweet daughter, I hope you'll always land on the positive side of the law of attraction. I hope you'll always see the glass half full and not half empty. I hope you'll never be lost, but only "off course."

Incidentally, that 1986 Chuck Norris film is called *Firewalker*, in case you ever want to see it. And, oh yeah, I produced it. Your uncle Ron once told me it was one of the best movies he had ever seen. Then again, he was courting your aunt Viv at the time, so it's possible he was mildly exaggerating. That's a different law of attraction altogether.

All my everlasting love,

Dad

# Thirty-Two: Evil

Dear Mackenzie,

Good and decent people find it very difficult to process the notion that evil exists in the world.

In July 2012, a gunman walked into a crowded movie theater in Aurora, Colorado, where a packed house had come to watch the newest installment in the *Batman* series. According to news reports, the gunman walked in, surveyed the theater and the people in it, and walked back out. Moments later he returned wearing full-body armor and holding a semiautomatic assault rifle and various other weapons. He tossed some tear gas canisters into the crowd and then opened fire.

By the time he exited the theater and waited by his car for police to arrest him, more than a dozen innocent people were dead and fifty more were injured. From what has been revealed so far, when the police went to the gunman's apartment, they found that it was booby-trapped with explosives designed to kill whoever walked through his door.

Once the police arrested him, ABC News called the man's mother in San Diego to get some information and confirm his identity. She didn't hesitate. "You have the right person," she told them.

"You have the right person"? I can imagine your mom saying all sorts of things in response to a call like that, Mackenzie, but "you have the right person" isn't in the universe of them. Did the killer's mother know of her son's proclivity for evil? Should or could she have done something about it if she did? I don't know. The mother later recanted the statement and said she had been quoted out of context.

The stories of the victims of the Aurora tragedy are beyond sad. Veronica Moser, who had gone to the movie with her pregnant mom, was only six years old when she died. Her mother is now paralyzed. Twenty-five-year-old Jon Blunk died when he heroically covered his girlfriend with his own body and the bullets hit him instead. He was one of three young men who died in this courageous fashion, saving someone they loved.

Jessica Ghawi had moved from Toronto, Canada, to Aurora less than a year earlier. The previous June, she had survived a killing spree in a mall in Toronto. She had written a blog post shortly thereafter commenting about "how fragile life is" and how lucky she was to be alive and able to pursue her dreams. She was twenty-four. The stories, and the tears, go on and on. What does it all mean?

The tragedy ignited yet another nationwide debate about gun control. Initial reports indicate that the gunman had bought the assault rifle, various other guns, explosives, and more than six thousand (!!!) rounds of ammunition, completely legally. Six thousand rounds, and no one raised an eyebrow.

Advocates of more stringent gun control laws believe that a perpetrator's ability to get such firepower so easily makes tragedies like this more common. They also argue that the Second Amendment is no longer relevant or necessary in today's world, because these days our militias are very well armed and prepared.

Opponents of gun control argue that "guns don't kill people; people kill people." They also argue that the Bill of Rights is sacrosanct, and that any attempt to curtail the right to bear arms must be met with the strictest of scrutiny.

Both sides are right. It's unlikely that if the founding fathers were writing the Constitution today, the right to bear arms would find its way into the Bill of Rights. It's hard to envision that an ordinary citizen's need to carry an AK-47 would be deemed as something warranting constitutional protection.

At the same time, it's too easy to simply lay blame for this horrible event at the feet of the NRA. This gunman was deliberate, malignant, and well prepared. Guns. Bombs. Tear gas. Dynamite. He had them all. With or without NRA protections, he would have found a way to act out and kill his prey.

The tragedy also reignited the debate about violence in movies and in the media generally. No doubt both sides of the debate will make worthwhile arguments. Similarly, experts on human psychology turned over everything from this guy's baby food to the information on his dating websites to try to make heads or tails of what went down and why.

What caused this highly intelligent young man with no known history of violence or trouble with the law to randomly go berserk on a group of innocent people? So far no one can tell.

What all of these debates missed is a simple and scary truth. Some people are simply evil and there is no rational explanation for their bad deeds. There are some 323 million people in the United States, all of whom have pretty much the same access as this killer to assault rifles, to tear gas, and to violent movies. Yet 99.9999 percent of them haven't shot up a movie theater, or a school, or a mall, or even a mouse.

As a society, we feel the need to analyze what happened from a thousand different angles, because we can't fathom that a being of our same species could possibly do something so horrible. But the fact that most of us can't comprehend this sort of pure evil is good news. It simply means most of us are not.

There is evil in the world, my sweet daughter. Ultimately neither gun control nor G-rated movies can defend against it. The most you can do is acknowledge it, try to stay out of its path, and hope it doesn't find you when you least expect it.

All my everlasting love,

Dad

# Thirty-Three:
# Happily Learning Absolutely Nothing

Dear Mackenzie,

When you get to be an adult, my sweet daughter, you'll find that the basic responsibilities of life never really go away. They don't even take much of a holiday. You'll have a job. A family. A mortgage. When you reach a certain age, these will become your constant companions.

That's not necessarily a bad thing, mind you. I love my family with all my heart. And though having a family carries with it a certain cost in terms of time, money, and the like, I wouldn't trade it, or all of you, for anything in the world. I know your mom feels exactly the same as I do, and hopefully you, Heather, and Jamie will all feel that way too once you have families of your own.

My job is often grueling. It's often very stressful. And especially in my chosen line of work, it's hard to truly leave the job or its various pressures behind even while on vacation. That said, on most days I find my job interesting, challenging, and exciting. As for the monthly mortgage…well, I guess everyone needs a place to live. It all goes with the territory of adulthood, and there's no way around it.

The problem with all of these adult responsibilities is that after a while they can skew your approach to the world around you. If you're not careful, you can start to view everything through the filter of all that rational, responsible thinking. Before you know it, your brain can push memories of the pure joy of not having a care in the world back to some distant corner of your subconscious mind.

The other night you were playing a game on your computer, and I randomly asked you whether you wanted to learn about some particular topic or other. "Dad," you said impatiently, "I'm on summer vacation. I don't want to learn anything." I was a bit taken aback by your response. So I explained that I understood you were on vacation from school, but that learning is a yearlong process and that the classroom that is life isn't limited to certain months of the year.

It seemed to take all your faculties to even retain civility in the face of my statement, and you looked at me like I was from Mars. "I refuse to learn anything about anything until the new school year begins," you told me in that fiercely strong-willed way that is uniquely yours. "Don't even think about trying to teach me anything new until then." Satisfied that you had stymied my inappropriate attempt to teach you something off-cycle, you turned your attention back to your computer and resumed whatever game you were playing.

The adult part of my brain had a viscerally adverse reaction to your statement. I wanted to challenge you on it and to suggest that your approach was irresponsible and shortsighted. I wanted to remind you that learning inspires confidence. I wanted to tell you that an education fosters a positive self-image. I wanted to instill in you the notion that the more you learn, the higher the chance of success and happiness you will have in life.

Yet you had dismissed me in such an adorable way, and with such conviction, that all I could do was laugh. I decided to let it drop for the time being, but thought that our exchange had given me an organic opportunity for a future teaching moment. I decided to come back to the conversation when you were done playing and give you the guidance you needed and deserved. In fact, I started writing one of my letters to you, about the importance of education.

But the more I thought about it and what you had said, the more I started to remember my own summers when I had been your age, and what they had meant to me. As a young boy, I couldn't wait for summer vacation and all that it held. I would count down the final days, hours, and minutes until the school year was out. The final bell on the last day of school proclaimed my freedom for the next several months.

Summer meant that I would have no responsibilities, no homework, absolutely no cares in the world. I could (and did) play baseball in the park near our house from early in the morning until late at night. I could go swimming in the local community pool with my friends. I could hang out, sleep out, sleep in, sleep over, watch television, play marbles, wait for the Uncle Marty's Ice Cream truck to come down our street, and do (or not do) anything else my heart desired.

I was a kid and it was summer and the world was my oyster. No one made me learn anything in particular, or do anything in particular, or read anything in particular, or be responsible to anyone in particular. In hindsight I realize that those carefree days were crucial to my cognitive and emotional development. Those carefree days allowed me to recharge my batteries for the school year to come. Those carefree days helped me to reconnect with the joyous innocence that most of us experience far too infrequently once we reach adulthood.

So as it turns out, Mackenzie, you were absolutely right. And I want you to experience that exhilarating lightness of being for as long as possible and as profoundly as possible. I hope you will be able to tap into your carefree inner child throughout your adult life.

To that end, I promise not to teach you a single thing for the entire summer. I promise to let you play, and sing, and generally wreak havoc all summer long to your heart's delight.

And if you absolutely must learn something, don't let me catch you doing it.

All my everlasting love,

Dad

# Thirty-Four: Bigotry

Dear Mackenzie,

The famous eighteenth-century Irish philosopher Edmund Burke once said that all that's necessary for the forces of evil to win in the world is for enough good people to do nothing. Well, Burke actually used the word "men" instead of "people," but in fairness to him, in the eighteenth century he would probably have been hanged on a rope if he had included women in his philosophizing.

But the fundamental issue behind Burke's statement hasn't changed in the past three centuries. What should we do when we witness injustice that doesn't directly impact us?

Up until 2015, only a handful of states recognized marriage between two people of the same sex. Gay marriage is now the law of the land, and the next generation probably won't even remember what all the fuss was about or why anyone was against it.

Through the prism of hindsight, society will likely view this episode in our history much the same way we now look back at the days when interracial marriage was illegal, or when women didn't have the right to vote. These days most people are hard pressed to articulate why there was even a debate about women having the right to vote, let alone a prohibition against it.

Years from now, the notion that two people who loved each other couldn't get married in most states of our great country because they both had the same private parts will seem crazy. Not so in 2012. That year it came to light that Dan Cathy, the CEO of a four-billion-dollar-a-year fast-food company called Chick-fil-A, was donating millions of corporate dollars to political groups that were actively lobbying against the legalization of gay marriage.

When that brouhaha started, Cathy issued a statement saying that Chick-fil-A's corporate purpose was "to glorify God by being a faithful steward of all that is entrusted to us. To have a positive influence on all who come in contact with Chick-fil-A." It's a lovely sentiment.

I'm not sure how glorifying God and having a positive influence give rise to embracing homophobia, but that might be splitting hairs. More to the point, I think if I had been on the board of Chick-fil-A when they were discussing corporate purpose, I might have suggested that the corporation would be better served by leaving God out of the equation and instead committing to sell more chicken. Then again, nobody asked me.

You and your sisters, and actually our whole family, had been eating Chick-fil-A for a long time. For better or worse, we think their food is delicious. So when the story broke, there was quite a debate in our household. Should we or shouldn't we boycott the chain?

We all acknowledged that Cathy was entitled to his beliefs and opinions. And though I certainly disagree with his views, I support his right to them and even to air them publicly. Nor does anyone begrudge him the right to donate money to the groups of his choosing. At the same time, did we want to help fund those donations by giving Chick-fil-A our money?

That was the question around our dinner table. One night you asked if we could go eat at Chick-fil-A. Your mom told you what Cathy was doing and how that could impact some of our friends, many of whom you knew. I explained that we didn't want to support a business that was donating no small measure of its profits to groups we felt were promoting hatred and injustice.

I could see on your face that you were clearly conflicted, and so I asked you how you felt about it all. With the purity of a ten-year-old child, you said that when you thought about how those donations could harm our friends, you didn't want to eat there. But that on the other hand, "their food was sooooo good."

And there's the rub, my sweet daughter. Cathy's financial contributions don't directly affect us in any way. And yes, Chick-fil-A's chicken is tasty. But should we ignore the injustice? Should we look the other way?

I can tell you that I've eaten my last Chick-fil-A meal. And yet, should I be imposing my personal beliefs on you?

The good news is that ultimately history will not remember Cathy kindly, if at all. His fate will be much like that of former Alabama governor George Wallace, who is best remembered as the man who stood in front of Foster Auditorium at the University of Alabama in 1963 to physically block Vivian Malone and James Hood from entering the university to enroll, for the simple reason that they were black. Fifty years later, he sounds positively backward.

In the meantime, you have a decision to make. Tasty chicken? Or standing by your principles? The choice is yours. Don't squander it.

All my everlasting love,

Dad

# Thirty-Five: The Color of Money

Dear Mackenzie,

When I was about ten years old, my parents took me to see the film *Mary Poppins*, based on a series of books that featured a magical nanny. In the film, Mary's employer, who is a banker, sings to his son about the value of money, and of investing his "tuppence" at the Fidelity Fiduciary Bank. I love that movie, my sweet daughter, and that particular song. But how important is it for a ten-year-old to save money, or to understand money management?

A couple of years ago we started giving you a weekly allowance. The truth is that as a practical matter, you didn't need one. Like many parents who are able, we provide you with all the necessities of life and then some.

Even if we hadn't, you've been blessed at a very young age with a successful acting career that's allowed us to put away quite a bit of money in your college fund. That said, your mom and I thought that giving you an allowance was a great way for you to start learning how to manage money in a safe environment. It's hard to make a catastrophic mistake on ten dollars a week.

We also debated whether or not to tie your allowance to your doing some chores around the house. We liked the idea of your starting to learn the value of money earned for services rendered. On the other hand, you've been working eight-hour days or longer on stage and on-screen alongside adult professionals since the age of seven. In that light, it seemed rather foolish to offer you a few dollars to clean your room.

Not that you're aware of your net worth. A year or so ago, you wanted to buy an iPad. One night at dinner you asked how much an iPad cost, and we told you we thought it was approximately five hundred dollars. You immediately started calculating how long you would have to save in order to buy one. When you realized that given your allowance, it would take a year or more to buy one even if you saved every penny, you started negotiating with me about matching funds.

I was enjoying the exchange tremendously, but after a while your sister Jamie got fed up with the discussion and suggested that you simply use the money you had in the bank and buy one right then. You looked at her like she was crazy. "What are you talking about?" you answered. "I don't have any money." It took all of our willpower to maintain a straight face, but the moment was so pure and genuine that I agreed to match your savings dollar for dollar until you reached your goal.

A former colleague of mine used what I thought was a wonderful tool to teach her young children the value of money. Whenever the family went out to a restaurant, she would have the kids check the math when the bill came. If the kids found that the restaurant had overcharged them, or had done the math wrong in any way, she would give the difference to the kids.

Her children loved the game, and every so often they got a bit of found money. In the meantime, looking at the bill gave them a sense of the reality of how much things cost ("Wow, four dollars for a Coke? That's half my allowance!"), so the concept of what they were spending became less ethereal. It's genius. I've suggested that game to you several times and so far you've not been interested.

The problem with the allowance we were giving you was that we didn't stick to the plan. You rarely did the chores you were supposed to do each week, yet we gave you your allowance anyway. Half the time we didn't even remember what chores we had asked you to do.

Then we'd forget to give you your allowance for weeks at a time. You, in turn, would forget to ask for it, because whenever you needed something we'd just buy it for you, so you were never short on cash. In the end, you, your mom, and I showed all the fiscal discipline of an Enron executive, and the allowance experiment was a bust. Finally, all of us forgot about it. I blame myself.

And then a few months later you approached us again. You suggested you would be willing to do chores around the house, but that your weekly allowance would have to be "a lot higher." I realized you were presenting us with an opportunity to do it right this time. I also realized you were becoming a great negotiator. And yet I was conflicted.

Should we just give you an allowance and let you be a kid? And why did you offer up the chores? Was it because your friends were doing it? Was it because you were craving responsibility? With you having offered it up, would it scar you if we said you didn't have to do the chores? My initial idea was to tell you that one of your chores would be to hug your daddy every week, but wait, what would *that* be teaching you?

I'm neither a child psychologist nor an economist, but I've come to believe chores for money at age ten is silly. You'll have plenty of time for the anxiety of financial pressures your entire adult life. Why start that anxiety now? I had an allowance as a kid. I think it served to make me less carefree, and I'm still not very good with money management.

Arghh, who the hell knows? I leave the tough decisions to your mother.

All my everlasting love,

Dad

# Thirty-Six: True Love

Dear Mackenzie,

We all grow up reading fairy tales about true love and happily ever after. What little girl hasn't fantasized that she's Snow White or Cinderella, saved by the magical kiss of her one true love? A young girl's imagining of her wedding day is the ultimate manifestation of the fairy tale.

As I approached my own wedding to your wonderful mom, lots of people started to weigh in with opinions. When it all got a little dicey, a friend of mine gave me good advice. "Never forget, Norm," he said, "your wedding day is for two people and two people only, the bride and her mother." It was a funny line, and probably true.

And what about guys? Well, boys don't acknowledge it as readily, but it turns out the fairy-tale effect applies to us too. We dream of being the handsome prince who slays the dragon and wins the kingdom, and whose valor and courage are rewarded with our very own fantasy princess.

For those of us who think we may not be handsome enough to be the right kind of leading man, or beautiful enough to be the right kind of leading lady, fear not. Meet Shrek and Princess Fiona, two green and ugly ogres who, despite their physical shortcomings, find each other and true love, and live happily ever after. Well, at least until the sequel sends them on a new adventure. There's a fairy tale for everybody.

On the other end of the spectrum, literature is full of tragic stories about star-crossed lovers who, unable to be with their one and only soul mate, decide life is not worth living.

The most famous of these is probably the story of two young lovers named Romeo and Juliet. They have to marry in secret because of a longstanding feud between his family and hers. Towards the end of Shakespeare's tragedy, Romeo thinks that Juliet has killed herself.

Devastated, Romeo buys poison from a local apothecary (something between the local pharmacist and the local drug dealer) and takes his own life. Juliet then awakens from her self-induced coma and, realizing that Romeo has killed himself for her, stabs herself to death so they can be together for all eternity.

Lancelot and Guinevere. Tristan and Isolde. Cleopatra and Marc Antony. By the way, Mackenzie, I hope one day you'll get to know these wonderful classics. They will undoubtedly make you cry, but they'll also move you and inspire you and titillate you.

Whether it's happily ever after or death by soul mate, these two sides of the same coin all seem to make the same point: that of the seven and a half billion people on this earth, there is one and only one person destined for each of us. Can that be possible? And if it is, what are the odds that we will find that person? (I know, I know, about one in seven and a half billion.) Those are some very long odds, to say the least.

But is that how it all works in the real world? Is there really only one person for each of us? I don't know.

Most people have a very difficult time finding a soul mate, specifically because they believe it's all supposed to happen magically. We've been raised to believe that when it's our turn, Cupid shoots his arrow of love and our Cinderella or Prince Charming magically appears. It's not that simple.

As you'll already know by the time you read this letter, I actually did find a soul mate. Yet if you reread my letter to you called "How I Met Your Mother," you'll know that it took me some twenty-plus years to marry her after I first laid eyes on her. Had I been smart enough when your mom and I first met to understand the importance of giving Cupid a helping hand, your mom and I might have gotten together much earlier. Or maybe that would have doomed our love. Who knows?

In the not-too-distant future, your heart will start to search for true love. You'll be tempted to make lists of the traits that make up your perfect mate. Try not to do that.

"He has to be funny," or "we should meet in a romantic way," or "he has to have a job" have little to do with love or the perfect mate. Well, having a job would be good.

You'll be tempted to think that if he is "the one," love will blossom on its own. That's not true. Cupid can shoot his arrows till the cows come home. Unless you are bold and courageous and willing to risk, Cupid's arrows may miss their mark.

You'll be tempted to listen to your friends when they tell you someone is right for you or wrong for you. There's nothing wrong with getting advice on love, but as the saying goes, the heart is a lonely hunter. Your friends may be well intentioned, but in the end, only what's in your heart and his truly matters.

Be open to all that the universe may bring your way, my sweet daughter. Relationships aren't always easy, but falling in love should be. Chemistry. Pheromones. Swooning. Those elements are all crucially important. If your new love doesn't take your breath away every so often, that person may not be the one for you. But pheromones and chemistry are only part of the equation.

Your mom's sparkly green eyes make me swoon, but so does her kindness. Her touch takes my breath away, but so does her love of you and your sisters. Listen to your heart. Pay attention to the signals your body sends you. Look inside your soul.

And don't give short shrift to those things about a person that only being together over time can reveal. For in the end, whether it's Snow White and Prince Charming, Shrek and Fiona, Romeo and Juliet, or Norman and Laura, that is the stuff true love is made of.

All my everlasting love,

Dad

# Thirty-Seven:
# The Day I Almost Died in Morocco

Dear Mackenzie,

A few years ago I accompanied a client to Morocco, where he was being honored at the Marrakech International Film Festival. As it happened, my client was friends with the royal family, so we were literally treated like kings.

Among other things, we were assigned a palace car and driver, and were accompanied at all times by an armed guard, whom I'll call Fayiz (not his real name). Fayiz made no attempt to hide the huge gun he carried. He was friendly and respectful, and he was also very badass in the best sense of the word. Fayiz spoke decent English, and he and I became fast friends.

The traffic in Marrakech is very congested (picture Los Angeles traffic at…well, at any time), and I started to notice that our driver didn't even pretend to obey the rules of the road. He would run red lights, go the wrong way down one-way streets, and blatantly ignore the local police. Finally I asked Fayiz about it, and he told me that the car's palace insignia basically gave its driver carte blanche on the road. It was a little scary, but it was heady stuff too.

After a few days in Marrakech, we embarked on a driving tour of Morocco. With Fayiz and the royal car as part of our entourage, we continued to be treated like royalty even as we got farther and farther away from the city. Finally we arrived at a beautiful desert area called Ouarzazate.

I had to fly out to attend a meeting in New York, but my client wasn't ready to head back. So our guides arranged a local flight for me out of Ouarzazate. I would take the

6:00 AM commuter flight to Casablanca, where I would catch a connecting flight to NYC. We left the hotel late, but Fayiz told me he would accompany me to the airport and that I shouldn't worry.

Our driver was going about 110 miles per hour. Fayiz mistook my ashen look for concern about the time, so he told me he had called ahead to let the airport know we were on our way. Whatever that meant.

We arrived at the airport ten minutes after my flight was scheduled to depart. Fayiz calmly walked me to the ticket counter and exchanged a few words with the salesperson, after which she handed me a boarding pass without asking me for ID.

At security, Fayiz flashed his gun and his credential and proceeded to set off the metal detector. As the local police stood and watched, Fayiz waved me through, and though I wasn't carrying a gun, I set it off too. The local authorities looked at me strangely but did nothing. This was fun.

At the gate a lone airline employee stood next to the closed boarding door. Fayiz spoke to the guy, who unlocked the boarding door and waved me through. Fayiz smiled like a proud papa, and I leaned in to give him a big hug. He stepped back, but then laughed and hugged me back. I told him I hoped to see him again one day and boarded the plane.

I was the only Caucasian among the thirty or so passengers in various traditional Arab garments, plus a few people in conventional business attire. Everyone looked at me curiously. Who was this foreigner who'd had the juice to hold a plane in Morocco?

Once we were airborne, I sat back to reflect on the morning's events. At one point an announcement in Arabic seemed to make several of the passengers anxious. I didn't understand a word of it.

A flustered flight attendant rushed through the cabin shortly after, and people started shouting at him in Arabic. He didn't break stride, but he shouted back as he went. I knew that many people in Morocco speak French, so in halting French I asked the person across from me what was going on. Mind you, my sweet daughter, I speak very little French, but I was sure that what he answered was, "We are going down." As if on cue, the oxygen masks popped down in the cabin.

In the collective panic that was overtaking the flight, I could tell the plane was descending quickly and erratically. As I put the mask over my face, I was gripped by the notion that I would never see you or the rest of our family again. I could not believe that my life was going to end somewhere in the middle of North Africa. I prayed that God would look after you, your sisters, and your mom. I remember asking myself what I might have done better in my life. A woman behind me started to weep uncontrollably.

Another announcement came over the intercom that I didn't understand, but everyone went into the emergency landing position, so I did the same. Then I closed my eyes and waited.

After what seemed like an eternity but was probably no more than twenty or thirty seconds, the plane hit the ground very roughly, bounced around for a bit, and then started to taxi normally. People started looking around as the realization dawned that we had survived. A few people clapped. The guy across from me smiled and in very bad English said what I understood to be "See, we're on the ground." Or maybe he said, "May Allah abound." Either way was good with me.

A few minutes later we deplaned and were guided to some sort of bus to transport us to the terminal. While we were in the vehicle, a cell phone started to ring. An Arabic man reached into his *thawb*, pulled out a cell phone, and had a hushed conversation. I swear by everything that's holy this is what happened next.

The man looked up, walked over to me, and said, "Norman"? I nodded, and he handed me his cell phone. When I spoke into the phone, I heard the unmistakable voice of Fayiz. "Are you okay?" he asked. "We heard what happened and were worried about you."

To this day I have no idea what was wrong with that plane, but I know three things. I know that I'm happy to be alive to tell you this story. I know that some higher power was looking out for me that day. And I know that Fayiz is one badass dude.

All my everlasting love,

Dad

Los Alamos National Laboratory
of the University of California

Los Alamos, New Mexico 87545

May 19, 1993

Mr. Norm Aladjem
White House Advance Office
The White House
Washington, D.C. 20500

Dear Norm:

On behalf of the staff of the Laboratory and the people of Los Alamos, please accept my gratitude for your dedicated efforts in connection with President Clinton's recent visit.

So many people were impressed with your professionalism, your skill, and your spirit of cooperation that we will long remember your role in making the President's trip here an absolute success. My special thanks!

With appreciation,

S. S. Hecker
Director

SSH/avt

A LETTER OF THANKS FROM THIS VERY EVENT

FAST FORWARD TWENTY-FIVE YEARS, TO 2017

# Thirty-Eight:
# Sharing the Secrets of History

Dear Mackenzie,

Not long ago I watched former president Bill Clinton give an amazing speech. His presidency had many rocky moments, my sweet daughter, but these days Clinton is the distinguished gray eminence of the Democratic Party, and his command of the world stage is legendary. His speech took me back to his salad days when Clinton was first running for president, and to the very private exchange he and I once had in Los Alamos, New Mexico. It happened like this.

I'd always had an interest in politics, so in early 1992 I called a friend who worked for our local city councilman and asked him how I could get meaningfully involved in a political campaign. Without hesitation he told me to go to the nearest headquarters of any candidate about whom I was passionate and start licking envelopes.

With the benefit of hindsight, I realize my friend gave me great advice. In many ways political campaigns are the truest of meritocracies. Because campaigns have little time and even less money, for the most part all anyone cares about is whether you can get the job done. You can be licking envelopes today and be the deputy campaign manager tomorrow.

I didn't know that then, of course, and in my arrogance I thought licking envelopes was beneath me. I thanked my friend for the advice, told him I would take it under advisement, and asked him to keep me in mind if anything interesting came across his desk.

Sure enough, a few weeks later my friend called. "Governor Clinton is coming to Southern California on a campaign trip," he said, "and they need volunteers to drive staff vans in the motorcade." In those days I barely knew who Clinton was, but I thought it could be a fun way to spend a day. I felt very important when someone in Arkansas called me to get information for my FBI background check since I was going to be "in proximity to the candidate."

The night before Clinton was to arrive, someone on his advance team called me to say they couldn't use me as a driver. Before I could voice my disappointment, he said, "But we have the perfect job for someone with your skill set. We want you to oversee press movement at the event." I didn't think to ask how he could possibly know what my skill set was, and I excitedly agreed.

What I didn't know was that the press movement volunteer is simply the person who holds up a big sign that says "Press follow me." He was certainly right that I had the necessary skill set. I have two arms and two legs.

As instructed, I arrived the next day at 7:00 AM at the appointed location, wearing a suit and tie. A sign on the wall welcomed Governor Clinton "at 4:00 PM today." It was already about eighty degrees, and I saw only one person at the site. He was in shorts and a T-shirt and was setting up folding chairs.

I approached him very officiously and told him I was looking for Josh King, the lead site person for the event. He looked me up and down and said, "I'm Josh." I told him I was there to do press movement. "You'll be perfect for that," he said without missing a beat. "In the meantime, why don't you take off your coat and tie and help me set up."

Over the years, Josh has become a good friend, and he and I advanced numerous trips together. On that day, Josh made sure I had a lot of fun, and then set me up to go to Little Rock for training as a presidential advance person. Then I went on the road. After two or three advance trips, the campaign sent me to advance a trip Clinton was taking to Los Alamos. It was my first time being in charge of one of the sites the candidate was visiting, and I was very nervous.

Over the four days before Clinton arrived, I probably slept an aggregate of ten hours, which is probably about par for a presidential advance team. I learned my site inside and out. I memorized the names and titles of all the executives and all the politicos Clinton would meet while he was there. I coordinated with the Secret Service ad nauseam.

As the motorcade sped toward my site on the big day, the advance person in the car with Clinton hit me on the walkie-talkie. "We're seven minutes out." I was excited and ready for my big moment. "Four minutes out," the walkie-talkie crackled a couple of minutes later. "And Norm, Eagle (or whatever Clinton's code name was at that time) wants to talk to you privately the moment we arrive."

What? Why in the world would he need to talk to me privately? What could I possibly have done wrong already? I had met Clinton a few times on previous trips, but I was reasonably certain he had no idea who I even was. "He wants to talk to me?" I gasped. "Yes, he wants a word with you privately. One minute out."

For the life of me I couldn't figure out what I was supposed to do or say when I saw him. I braced myself for the worst, took my position where Eagle's car would stop, and resolved to enjoy what, for reasons unknown, seemed likely to be my last advance trip. The motorcade came around the bend and rolled toward me. Had I not been so scared, it would have been an exhilarating moment. The motorcade came to a stop, the door opened, and Clinton climbed out of the car.

"Norm?" he drawled. "Yes, Governor," I answered. "How may I be of service?" And then Eagle, who towered over me, put his arm around me like we'd known each other our whole lives and started guiding me away from the car so no one could overhear us. "Where's the men's room?" he whispered.

Such are the secrets of history.


All my everlasting love,


Dad

# Thirty-Nine: This Day of Atonement

Dear Mackenzie,

If you've read my letter to you on faith, you know that in many ways I'm conflicted about the various organized religions. Who's right? Who's wrong? Who knows?

For better or worse, your mom and I both grew up in Jewish households, and that's the religion we were taught. Though truth be told, we're not the most observant family, and I can't even say I know all that much about Judaism.

If you ask me about Purim, I'm far more likely to tell you about the delicious hamantaschen cookies your great-grandmother used to make than I am to tell you about Haman the Agagite, who tried to exterminate the Jewish people. Simchat Torah? Not a clue. Yet even the least observant in our faith are conversant with our two highest holy days, Rosh Hashanah, the Jewish New Year, and Yom Kippur, the Day of Atonement.

According to Jewish tradition, or at least Wikipedia, God inscribes each person's fate for the coming year into the Book of Life on Rosh Hashanah, and waits until Yom Kippur to seal the verdict. During the intervening days culminating in Yom Kippur, a Jewish person tries to amend his or her behavior and seeks forgiveness for wrongs done against God and against other human beings. On Yom Kippur we fast from sundown to sundown, we pray, we atone for our sins, and we hope that we are forgiven by God.

One of the few things I do remember from going to Sunday school as a kid is the apocryphal story that on Yom Kippur, a rabbi stands before God and has the following conversation:

"Have you studied all you should?" God asks the rabbi. "No," the rabbi replies.

"Have you prayed all you should?" God asks the rabbi. "No," the rabbi replies again.

Then God asks the rabbi a third question, "Have you done all the good you should toward your fellow congregants?" Yet again the rabbi admits he has not.

And God proclaims, "But you have told the truth, and for the sake of truth you are forgiven. Go forth in my name and make amends."

I've often wondered why this particular parable has stuck with me when so many others have not. I think it's because at bottom it quintessentially speaks to our humanity. Most of us mean well. Most of us make promises and vows to ourselves and to each other. Yet in daily life we fall short again and again. Our best traits as people are manifested when we can acknowledge our shortcomings, yet at the same time we can reach for a higher plane.

A friend of mine once told me that when she was growing up in the Catholic Church, she was taught by her priest that to repent actually meant to rethink. How very Jewish. Imagine, Mackenzie, a day set aside to rethink your values, to rethink how you might have treated people better in the past year, and to rethink how you can treat them better going forward. Imagine a day set aside simply to rethink how to live each day with increasing grace.

So here I sit on Yom Kippur atoning for my sins of the past year.

I ask myself how I can be a better husband and a better father and a better friend. I pray for God's guidance, though I wonder how God can possibly hear my prayers over the loud growling of my stomach.

I resolve to treat others better. I promise to be more patient. I commit to take the time to savor the magical moments in my life and to ignore the little annoyances. And mostly I thank God for you and for Jamie and for Heather, and of course for your wonderful mom. I reflect on how truly blessed I am in my life.

And finally, I wonder what Yom Kippur could possibly mean to you as an eleven-year-old. The answer comes around lunchtime, when you ask me if I will buy you a sandwich from Subway. I explain to you everything I know about Yom Kippur, and about atonement, and about why in the Jewish tradition we fast on this day. You listen to me patiently and politely until you're sure that I am done. And then you look at me and say, "But Daddy, I'm really hungry. Aren't you?"

I'm probably not the best father on the planet. Lord knows I'm not the best Jew. And while I'll be the first to acknowledge I don't know much, I do know this. At least in this life, and for as long as I am able, when my little daughter is hungry, I'm going to make sure she gets fed.

I hope God can forgive me.

And yes, I'm hungry too, my sweet daughter. I plan to eat right after sundown.

All my everlasting love,

Dad

# Forty: Facing Adversity

Dear Mackenzie,

A man gets shipwrecked on a deserted island. Every day he scans the horizon hoping to be rescued, but help never comes. He's despondent and fears he's going to die in this godforsaken place. To protect himself from the elements, the man builds a little hut for himself out of driftwood. One day while he's out scavenging for food, he sees smoke rolling up to the sky from the direction of his hut. He runs to the hut only to find it engulfed in flames.

The man is stunned as he watches his last hope for survival burn to the ground. He's overcome with grief and anger at the notion that all is lost, and he cries himself to sleep. Early the next day, however, he is awakened by the sound of a ship that has come to rescue him. "How did you know I was here?" the weary man asks his rescuers. "We saw your smoke signal," they answer.

So far you've been very blessed throughout your young life. Other than maybe not getting an acting role or two that you may have wanted, or having to do schoolwork when you'd rather be at Disneyland, you haven't experienced much in the way of hard times. And if your mom and I could have our way, bad luck and trouble would never find you.

Unfortunately, there's not much we can do to shield you from such things. At some point you may be challenged in your career. You may stumble in your personal life. Maybe you'll face financial challenges. In fact, sooner or later all these things may find themselves at your door.

The urge to give up when the going gets tough is only human. Uncertainty creates anxiety, and the fear of pain trumps the desire for pleasure in virtually every instance. So what should you do to keep from giving up when nothing is going right?

Below are Dad's three rules for overcoming adversity in your personal and business life. Ready?

Rule number one: When things don't go right, immediately assess and acknowledge the situation you are in.

This is one of the hardest things for people to do in a crisis, but if you don't do it, you'll only dig a deeper hole for yourself. Your boyfriend left you? Assess and acknowledge the situation you are in. Your company is going under? Assess and acknowledge the situation you are in. You have a life-threatening illness? Assess and acknowledge the situation you are in. You can't solve any problem that you won't admit at least to yourself.

One day many years ago, I was on vacation in Hawaii when I got a call from the controller of the company I was working at. "What's up?" I asked him as I sipped my tropical drink. After a few seconds of silence, he spit out, "I thought I should tell you we can't meet payroll tomorrow." I thought I had misheard. Cash flow is cyclical in almost every business, which is why companies have revolving lines of credit. "Why don't you just go into our credit line?" I gamely suggested. "It's tapped out," he said. "I've been hoping collections would accelerate."

The controller had refused to assess and acknowledge that our receivables that quarter had not kept up with our expenses. Maybe he was embarrassed. Maybe he feared he would be blamed if he shined a light on the problem. Who knows? But without acknowledging what we were actually facing, he couldn't address the issue. Needless to say, he wasn't our controller much longer.

Rule number two: When things don't go right, tackle the issue that is directly in front of you without getting distracted by related problems not yet at your doorstep.

I once read a script in which two detectives, a rookie and a seasoned veteran, are trapped on the top floor of an abandoned building. Bad guys are shooting at them, and more bad guys await them on the stairwell and in the lobby. "How many do you reckon are on the stairwell?" the rookie asks his partner between rounds. "And how many do you reckon are in the lobby?" "Why don't we worry about staying alive for the next sixty seconds?" says his partner. "We'll know about the other guys soon enough."

However difficult what you face in life may be, Mackenzie, I can tell you with 100 percent certainty that you'll be able to deal with it more effectively if you can focus on the actual problem at hand. If you lose your job, for example, the challenge in front of you is to get another job. That's what you must make yourself tackle. It's true that if you don't get another job, you may lose your house. You may well feel humiliated in front of your family and friends at having been fired. Yet you must make yourself minimize those fears and feelings lest you get overwhelmed and derail the real task at hand.

Rule number three: When things don't go right, remember that the knot in your stomach is temporary.

The ultimate fact we must acknowledge is that not all problems are solvable. Loved ones die. Passion fades. The Cleveland Browns…well, you get the idea.

The untimely death of your grandma was a bitter pill for me to swallow, and I miss her every day. But as time goes by, the pain lessens, and the memories of her and of our time together fill my heart with warmth and love. When I was in my twenties and a romantic relationship ended, I was certain I'd never find love again. Yet I did find love, and years later I can barely remember some of the people who broke my heart. I guess I'm saying if you can imagine what the problem might look like to you from the rearview mirror, you'll be better able to handle it in the present.

All that said, my sweet daughter, may you never get shipwrecked on a desert island. But if you do, I hope this letter helps you build your hut.

All my everlasting love,

Dad

# Forty-One: Safeguarding the Rights of Idiots and Fools

Dear Mackenzie,

When I was in law school, I learned that the constitutional rights of the innocent are often reaffirmed on the backs of guilty people. Anyone who has ever watched a cop show on television, for example, is familiar with the notion of reading a suspect his or her Miranda rights.

In 1963, Ernesto Miranda was arrested for kidnapping and rape. He was convicted and sentenced to prison. His lawyers appealed. They argued that Miranda had not been told, among other things, that he had the right to an attorney, so his confession was improperly obtained. The U.S. Supreme Court agreed and overturned his conviction.

But make no mistake, my sweet daughter. Miranda was guilty as sin of the crimes for which he had been convicted. He was subsequently retried without the "tainted" confession, convicted, and served many years in prison. Yet Miranda's actual guilt or innocence was irrelevant to the Supreme Court. Their job was to protect his constitutional rights, and ours.

One of the most entertaining cases I studied in law school was *Cohen v. California*. By the mid-1960s, people were protesting heavily against the draft and against the Vietnam War. In 1968, Paul Robert Cohen was arrested for wearing a jacket inside a Los Angeles courthouse bearing the words "fuck the draft." He was convicted of disturbing the peace. The case wound its way through the court system, and the U.S. Supreme Court overturned the conviction, saying it violated Cohen's First Amendment rights.

Cohen's attorney at the Supreme Court was the late Melville Nimmer, a well-known constitutional scholar who just happened to be my First Amendment professor at UCLA. One of my favorite memories of law school is of Professor Nimmer lecturing our class about how he argued that case.

The prosecution's argument had rested on the theory that the words "fuck the draft" were incendiary and had a tendency to provoke others to commit violent acts or to disturb the peace. Professor Nimmer recounted to us that prior to oral argument, he had received strongly worded "advice" from clerks of the various Supreme Court justices that he was not to use the word "fuck" during oral argument. The court considered it "demeaning to the institution of the highest court in the land."

Professor Nimmer told us that he indeed feared if he said "fuck" during oral argument, some of the justices would hold it against him in deciding the case. As he prepared, however, he realized that although he might not win the case if he insulted the justices, his position rode on the notion that the words were constitutionally protected, even in front of the Supreme Court. As Nimmer put it, though, he was "fucked" either way.

The big day came, and Professor Nimmer stood in front of the nine justices. Before he could utter a single word, apparently one of the justices cautioned him yet again by welcoming him to the "dignified" and "respected" halls of the Supreme Court. What to do?

"Good morning," he began. "We are here to talk about the words 'fuck the draft.'" He relayed to us that several of the justices looked shocked and appalled as he repeated the phrase several times. Well, without getting into the legal arguments, let's just say that though guaranteeing fundamental freedoms can sometimes get messy, Professor Nimmer, and the First Amendment, ultimately won the day.

It's disappointing, however, when people use their fundamental rights to do stupid things. Not too long ago, someone posted on YouTube one of the most offensive short films you'll ever watch. It's called "Innocence of Muslims," and basically the video ridicules Islam generally and defames the prophet Muhammad specifically.

The film is so poorly made that but for the treatment of its subject matter, no one would have seen it or cared. The quality of the acting, writing, and directing is laughably bad. It's so bad, in fact, that when I went on YouTube myself to see what had caused such worldwide attention and anxiety, I initially thought I had mistakenly stumbled upon a spoof.

Yet the video instantly went viral, and garnered protests and violence around the world. It has been banned in more than a dozen Muslim countries. It has escalated hatred of America and the West.

The video and its aftermath are unique in two ways. First, the actors were apparently not told they were filming an anti-Islam film. No one was given a full script, nor was there any reference to Muhammad or to Islam during production. The actors were told they were shooting an action film, and all the religious references were dubbed in by the director-producer during postproduction.

Second, religious and special interest groups around the world immediately started spinning to serve their own purposes. First we heard that the film had been financed by Israeli Zionists bent on defaming Islam. Then it was reported that the film had instead been financed by a group of Egyptian Muslims bent on making the West look bad. Then it came out the film had been financed by an individual crackpot with an axe to grind. Who really financed the film and why? I don't know.

It's neither the first time nor the last that someone will use his or her fundamental rights to wreak havoc. I wish the person or group who made "Innocence of Muslims" had more sense. I wish the author or authors of the film had put their First Amendment rights to better use.

Mackenzie, I hope you'll treasure the fundamental rights that have been bestowed upon us by our founding fathers. They are hard fought and well earned. Yet I also hope you'll follow your grandma's advice: "If you have nothing nice to say, say nothing at all."

All my everlasting love,

Dad

# Forty-Two: Hubris

Dear Mackenzie,

Everybody makes mistakes.

It's part of the human condition, and it's nothing to be ashamed of. My own world-view, in fact, is that the more mistakes you make in life, the fuller and more vibrant your life can be. What you shouldn't do is make the same mistakes repeatedly, or for the wrong reason.

Hubris, though, is something else completely. Sad to say we're all susceptible to it at one point or another. By the time you read this letter, you may have studied the Greek myth about Icarus. Icarus was the son of Daedalus, an Athenian craftsman.

When Daedalus and Icarus were imprisoned by King Minos, Daedalus made two pairs of wings out of wax and feathers for himself and his son. Daedalus warned Icarus not to fly too close to the sun nor too close to the sea, but rather to follow his (Daedalus') path of flight.

Once they took off, Icarus was overcome by the godlike power he felt that flying gave him, and he started soaring higher and higher across the sky. But he got too close to the sun, the sun's rays melted the wax, and Icarus fell into the sea and drowned.

Nowhere in world history do we have better examples of hubris at work than in Napoleon Bonaparte's military campaign to conquer Russia in 1812 or Adolf Hitler's invasion of Russia in 1941. Note to people with hubris: stay out of Russia in the winter.

Napoleon was a great military leader and considered himself a strategic genius. He had conquered most of Europe by the time he turned his attention to bringing Russia to its knees. Napoleon had met Alexander I several years earlier, and the young Russian emperor had been in awe of the great Napoleon. They became allies, but when Russia reopened trade with Great Britain against Napoleon's wishes, Napoleon decided to teach Alexander a lesson and bring Russia to heel.

Napoleon was so arrogant and confident in his powers that he ignored the Russian weather, believing that he would defeat his enemy in one big, quick battle. The Red Army had other ideas. They continued to retreat strategically, drawing Napoleon and his army deeper and deeper into Russia. By the time the Russian Campaign was over, close to 400,000 French troops lay dead and Napoleon's aura of invincibility was over.

Having consolidated his power across much of Europe and Russia, Adolf Hitler mistakenly concluded that England was counting on Russia to enter the war on its side. Stalin (who had issues of his own) had been Hitler's partner in dismembering Poland, and the two countries had a nonaggression pact. Yet Hitler decided that if he knocked off Russia, England would lose hope and fold. So he ignored the Russian winters and invaded. Thankfully for the world, that, and other arrogant blunders, cost Hitler the war and ultimately his life.

Hubris isn't limited to military leaders, of course.

Hubris made Bernie Madoff think he could openly bilk investors out of billions of dollars, and it caused the collapse of Enron, Bear Stearns, and a host of other financial institutions.

In 1978, hubris caused a pitcher from Allegheny College to decide to pitch to me in the bottom of the ninth with first base open and the winning run on second base.

Many years ago my good friend Phillip Muhl invited me to lunch. He wanted me to meet an acquaintance of his named Sheryl who was trying to break into the entertainment industry. The three of us had a nice meal while she talked about some jingles she had recorded and how she wanted to get a record deal.

I had just left the practice of law and was in the middle of producing a film. I was on top of the world and way too big for my britches. At some point during the lunch, Phillip suggested that maybe I should manage her. Very full of myself, I dismissively responded that she should send me a demo tape, and I told her I would call her after I'd had a chance to review her material. I did give Sheryl some general advice about the business, mostly to make myself feel important.

I no longer remember if her demo was any good or if I even listened to it, but I do know that I never followed up with her. All these years later, Phillip still likes to rib me about how I passed on representing Sheryl, whose last name just happened to be Crow and who somehow went on to have an extraordinary career without me.

Well, some lessons you have to learn the hard way.

All my everlasting love,

Dad

# Forty-Three: Checking Out of the Hotel Transylvania

Dear Mackenzie,

A couple of months ago, your mom and our friend Cheramie, whose daughter Madison played Annie in the 2008–2009 national Broadway tour of *Annie*, decided to organize a reunion of that touring company in New York City. They coordinated it to coincide with a performance of the latest *Annie* revival on Broadway. Everyone would get together for dinner and then go see the Broadway show. The event would take place on Saturday, October 27, 2012.

The night before the reunion, you asked me if I would take you to see the animated movie *Hotel Transylvania*, which was playing on 42nd Street not too far from our apartment. I had no idea what the film was about and didn't care. I was excited about having some father/daughter bonding time.

To my delight, you held my hand as we walked down Eighth Avenue all the way to the movie theater. Not wanting to press my luck, I didn't comment on it, but I remember thinking how great it would be if I could bottle that moment and hold on to both you and it forever. Watching your child grow up in front of your eyes, as any parent will tell you, is fraught with conflicting feelings, to say the least.

Ironically enough, *Hotel Transylvania* is about that very thing. The film tells the story of Count Dracula, the owner of a hotel where the world's monsters can take refuge from human civilization and the perils of "the outside world." In the film, we learn that the love of Dracula's life was murdered by a mob of angry humans. As a result, Dracula is desperate to make sure that his daughter, Mavis, never leaves the safety of the hotel.

He provides Mavis with all the love, creature comforts, and great birthday parties that any monster could ever need. But of course, all Mavis wants to do for her 118th birthday is to leave the nest and experience the world for herself. Hijinks ensue, and Daddy Dracula learns a valuable lesson about parental love.

Which brings me back to the reunion. About twenty members of the *Annie* touring company, including assorted "orphan" moms, dads, and grandmas, had dinner in Midtown before the show. As food and drink flowed, I watched as Analisa (Grace Farrell), Lynn (Miss Hannigan), Jillian (Star-to-Be), Zander (Rooster Hannigan), Cy (ensemble), and Sari (swing) shared their stories of the road. At the next table, Madison, Jordan, Siara, Sydney, and you (the orphans) laughed and shrieked like long-lost siblings.

At one point someone yelled out the word "Miami," and everyone hooted and hollered at the memories. Anchorage came up, and the stories flowed about the volcano that had erupted while the company was in Alaska. On it went like that throughout the meal.

After dinner we went to the show, where Liz, Kelly, Kenny, Patrick, and Dustin joined us. The performance was just fine, and hopefully Broadway will have another big hit.

But watching the show was a mixed experience for me, and probably for much of our group. I suspect that most of the company saw the production either through the filter of their own interpretation of the same roles or, like me, through the prism of memories of their young child onstage. I choked up at all the places where I used to choke up during the tour. Whoever the young girl playing Molly was, I never saw her. I saw only you.

When the show was over and the audience was gone, we all went up onstage and took a few group pictures for posterity with Sandy the dog. No one was ready for the night to end, so we went for a late bite and another drink or two, and had a few more laughs remembering the good old days.

The evening wore on, and eventually people started peeling off to return to the real world and their present-day lives. The group dwindled, and amidst hugs and maybe a tear or two, everyone promised to get together again soon. Who knows? We might even do it. Walking back to the apartment, I couldn't help but be amazed by this special group of friends.

*Hotel Transylvania* was still fresh in my mind too, and I was learning about letting go. I had to fly out early the next morning and knew you'd still be sleeping when I left, so I started to say goodbye to you in a manner befitting the young woman you're fast becoming.

You responded by grabbing me into a deep hug, and we held each other like that for about a minute, with neither of us saying a word. Now a minute is an awfully long time to be in a hug, my sweet daughter. But in the emotional universe of a daddy holding on to his little girl, I can tell you it goes by in a millisecond.

I don't know what was going through your mind during that minute, but in that wonderful hug I got clarity. Soon enough you'll be checking out of your own Hotel Transylvania. That's the natural order of things. We couldn't stop you even if we wanted to, and ultimately we want to encourage you to spread your wings.

Yet the notion of you eventually leaving doesn't mean that we can't savor every moment of the stay. And we should record wonderful memories in our mind's eye that, like with the *Annie* experience, we can share with each other over and over as the years go by.

I may even ask for a late checkout.

All my everlasting love,

Dad

# Forty-Four: The Miracle of Aunt Viv

Dear Mackenzie,

Your aunt Viv is one of the most decent people I've ever met. She's kind. She's giving. She loves unconditionally and profoundly. She has a strong faith in God. And she believes in miracles.

About three or four years ago, your aunt Viv got very sick. Something was wrong with her lungs, and no one could figure out what the problem was. As her illness wore on and after discarding several of the more benign possibilities, the doctors thought Viv must have some form of lung cancer. We waited with our hearts in our throats for the test results, fearing the worst. Only Viv held steadfastly to the notion that God was with her and that this was not her time to go.

While we were waiting for the test results, your grandpa, who is a very seasoned doctor, went to see Viv in the hospital. Afterward he called me. "I'll be very surprised if she has cancer," he said. When I asked him why, he said she was not showing the physical indications of someone with lung cancer. I couldn't tell you how he described it medically, but in layperson terms she was simply doing better, which your grandpa said is not how the body behaves as lung cancer progresses.

Sure enough, a battery of tests showed no sign of lung cancer, or of any other cancer, for that matter. Viv's health continued to improve, and other than some scar tissue in her lungs, the doctors declared that she was cured. They said her illness had been "idiopathic," which is medical jargon for "we don't know what the hell caused it or why it stopped." Viv had a different explanation. God had performed a miracle.

I'm not the most devout person, nor the most pious. But in the face of what we had just witnessed, I had to acknowledge that a miracle had indeed occurred. We celebrated life, God, and our good fortune, and left it at that.

Then about a year later, Viv started getting pneumonia with alarming frequency. Back to the doctors she went. More tests, more theories, more diagnoses. And slowly a consensus began to build amongst the specialists that Viv had something called interstitial lung disease, a chronic disease that manifests with increasing scarring of the lungs. At some point it becomes irreversible and terminal.

As Viv's health continued to deteriorate, I privately came to reframe the miracle as simply a misdiagnosis. To this day I haven't been able to shake the notion that a better team of pulmonary specialists might have figured things out earlier and been able to help her while the disease was still in its infancy. Who knows? But does that mean God isn't at Viv's side, or that her life hasn't been blessed with miracles? Not at all.

Your aunt Viv got married a bit later in life, and she was blessed with a marriage most people only dream of. Your uncle Ron is her best friend and soul mate. The two have been by each other's side through thick and thin, and they remain solidly, unshakably, dare I say divinely, in love. Viv always wanted a big family, and their beautiful blended one is chock-full of children and grandchildren whom they love and who love them.

Viv is a healer. She's also a natural leader, a writer, and a public speaker. She had a wonderful career as an obstetrical nurse. She has led the nursing corps of various ob-gyn units. She has given seminars on leadership and on nursing all over the country. I can tell you, my sweet daughter, that those things fulfilled her and made her incredibly happy. I never saw Viv more giddy with joy than when she was staying in some little motel in the middle of nowhere, teaching a seminar or making a speech. Maybe I'm crazy, but being able to do the things one loves to do while making a difference in the world, well, isn't that a miracle?

Although our family was Jewish, in her twenties your aunt Viv converted to Christianity. I never asked her what had brought her to that epiphany, but her newfound faith fortified her and made her happy, and she found comfort in God's hands.

So was her idiopathic illness and temporary cure of a few years ago a miracle? I have no idea. A miracle may not be explicable by natural or scientific laws, but unfortunately interstitial lung disease is. And barring some sort of medical miracle now, your aunt Viv will shortly transition from this earthly existence to whatever may be next.

The real miracle, though, the sustaining miracle, the miracle I will remember all the days of my life, is the goodness and the light and the love that is your Aunt Viv. No one who has known her will forget the bigness of her heart, or her ability to face adversity with the utmost grace, or the legacy that is evident when one simply looks around at her family.

Whoever God is, wherever God roams, whatever His plan, may He look after your aunt Viv for all eternity in the way that she so richly deserves.

Amen.

All my everlasting love,

Dad

# Forty-Five: Your High School Years

Dear Mackenzie,

The other day your mom asked me if I thought we should attend our high school reunion next year in Cleveland. The answer for me was a quick and easy yes. Was she crazy? Who wouldn't want to go to his high school reunion with the "It" girl on his arm?

The conversation started me thinking about you, though, and about your upcoming high school years. You've been home-schooled or schooled on sets since you were in first grade. Initially when we started homeschooling you, I had grave reservations. I wasn't too worried about the three Rs. I felt reasonably comfortable that you could learn all of that in due course.

What did worry me was whether homeschooling would affect your social development. I'd heard all the horror stories about how the social skills of homeschooled children lag behind because they aren't exposed to classrooms and schoolyards, and all the life lessons those settings foster.

As it turns out, it appears I needn't have worried. Four years into your homeschooling you're socially adept and then some. You're good with kids your own age and with older kids too. You can hold your own with adults, and though you're only eleven, I've rarely seen you in a situation in which you weren't comfortable in your own skin.

I don't know whether your social skills will endure as you get older. I hope they do. Conversely, I worry whether the one thing I didn't fret over, the three Rs, will come back to be the real problem as time goes by. Hopefully it will all turn out okay. So far, so good.

But what about the high school experience itself? What will you be able to reminisce about years later that will bring a tear to your eye and a smile to your face?

I certainly don't mean the classes. I'm hard pressed to point to a single high school class that sent me in an interesting academic direction, and I can't even remember the name of any of my high school teachers. In fairness, that may be more a reflection of me than of the institution. Your aunt Viv says I've blocked out much of my childhood. She may be right.

I do remember, though, that one day during my junior year at Cleveland Heights High School, our chemistry teacher gave us a pop quiz about the periodic table. We all thought we had done poorly. The next day as the bell rang to end the class, the professor asked me to stay behind for a minute.

I thought I might be in trouble, but when the rest of the kids emptied out and we were alone, the teacher turned to me with that sympathetic yet dry tone that doctors use when they give patients very bad news. "Norm," she said softly, "you seem like a nice young man, and I want to help guide you."

I didn't really know where this was heading and I must have been staring at her blankly, because she ratcheted up her sympathetic tone. "College isn't for everyone," she continued. "There are some fine vocational schools that can teach you a craft to get by in the world. Perhaps you could be a diesel mechanic...or maybe even a plumber."

I grant you that I didn't have the most distinguished high school academic career, my sweet daughter. But can you imagine the damage that kind of uninformed comment can inflict on a young mind? I shudder to think how many kids' lives that teacher may have inadvertently sent in a wrong direction. No doubt as I write you this letter, some knucklehead shop teacher somewhere is probably telling the next Jimmie Johnson he should quit wasting his time with race cars and go to dental school.

So no, I'm not at all concerned about your missing out on the classroom experience. But as you get older, I do want you to have all the same types of wonderful memories that your mom has about her high school years, and that I have about mine. How do you amass memories like those if you're homeschooled? I'm not sure.

I remember driving around aimlessly on Saturday nights listening to the radio and looking for trouble with my friend Howie, who now calls himself Howard and deals with presidents and prime ministers, and my friend Vic, who now calls himself Victor and performs high-risk cardiac surgeries.

I remember Coach Lieberman telling me I was too small to play high school baseball and running me ragged practice after practice trying to get me to quit the team, and then after the season telling me he thought I had become one of the best defensive center fielders in the state.

I remember Nina Fromer, who fueled my fascination with pretty Israelis.

I remember Randy Stoner (not his real name—here's why) taking me to an abandoned building one day after school and offering to share his joint with me. I coughed and hacked and then told him the weed had no effect on me, after which I stopped off at the local deli and ate two packs of Twinkies because I had the munchies.

I remember Harvey Kirshenbaum and Elizabeth Buck and Scott Comp and John Ernest, all of whom were taken too soon.

And of course, I remember the beautiful "It" girl.

Those are the memories that fill my heart. Whether you ultimately go to a regular high school or are homeschooled through your high school years, in the end the memories you create will be uniquely yours.

If your memories give you as much joy and delight through the prism of time as mine have given me, you'll be one very lucky girl indeed.

All my everlasting love,

Dad

# Forty-Six:
# The Moment before the Moment

Dear Mackenzie,

At 5:56 PM on Friday, November 16, 2012, I got a call at work from your sister Jamie. I'd given my assistant strict instructions that afternoon to put Jamie through no matter what I was doing when she called, but the timing was off. I was expecting the call at 6:01 PM and not a minute before. "I'm shaking and I can't stop crying," she said when I picked up. "Can you stay on the phone with me for a few minutes?"

We chatted about this and that; the topics didn't really matter. Jamie just needed for time to pass. At exactly 6:00 PM, Jamie said she'd call me back, and jumped off.

I'd been there before. We all have. Jamie was experiencing that excruciating phenomenon known as the moment before the moment. I knew I'd be hearing from her again shortly, so I didn't want to get on another call. Instead, my mind wandered to an excruciating "moment before" that I myself experienced in June of 1999.

Your mom and I had been dating for about seven months, and we had planned a vacation together. At the time, your mom was living in Philadelphia and I was in Los Angeles, so we decided to meet up in New York and fly to Europe from there. Unbeknownst to your mom, I also planned to ask her to marry me.

Of course that presented certain questions. Should I propose to her in New York? Or should I wait until we got to Europe and propose to her among the ancient ruins of Rome, one of the most romantic cities on earth?

There was much debate among my friends. My more passionate friends favored the eternal city. My practical friends worried about my losing the ring, or about your mom finding it prematurely, and so favored New York. My most cynical friend asked the searing question: "What if she says no?"

I didn't think your mom would say no, my sweet daughter. But then again, you don't know for sure until you ask the question. I decided to propose to her in New York, but I wanted to make the moment as romantic and memorable as possible.

I knew Central Park pretty well, because I had organized a big event there for the World Cup, and I remembered a beautiful secluded area near Sheep Meadow that I thought would provide the perfect setting. I intended to propose to her there and then take her on a carriage ride around the park.

My friend John Moeller had worked with me on the World Cup and was very connected in the city. So he arranged for a beautiful carriage, stocked with champagne and chocolate-covered strawberries, to meet us at a predetermined location at the park entrance. The driver would be holding a bouquet of yellow flowers so I could identify him. As it turned out, I didn't need the identifying flowers, but I did have to convince the driver that we were in fact the couple he was there to escort.

Anyway, that was in the days before texting and smartphones, so very late the night before, I made up some excuse to leave the hotel room for a minute so I could confirm that the carriage was in place. Apparently I wasn't a very polished liar, and months later your mom confessed that when I left the room that night, she feared I was calling another woman!

The next morning, I suggested we go to the Starbucks near the park. I had the engagement ring in my pocket and a knot in my stomach. When we walked outside it was drizzling, but I was determined to carry out my plan. To my relief, your mom followed my lead.

We strolled into the park and of all things, the area I had in mind was roped off. Your mom must have thought I was nuts as I kept walking her around the park trying to improvise the perfect spot. Finally we came upon a clearing with a little bench in it, and it was deserted except for a homeless guy nearby.

The rain was picking up, and I walked your mom over to the bench. My heart was pounding and my mouth was dry. I took a deep breath, held her hand in mine, got down on bended knee, told your mom I loved her and wanted to spend the rest of my life with her, and asked her to marry me.

The moment before the moment. I held my breath and waited for her answer. We stayed frozen like that for an eternity, which in real time was no more than a second or two. The homeless guy gave me a very sympathetic look. Finally your mom said, "Get up, honey. Your pants are getting dirty."

I was lifted from my reverie by my assistant, who poked his head in to tell me Jamie was again on the phone. It was 6:01 PM. The moment before had given way to the actual moment. My heart jumped to my throat but I said, "Hi, sweetheart," as casually as I could muster.

I heard the lightness in her voice, and in that instant I knew Jamie had passed the California bar exam. I congratulated her and told her how proud I was of her. We spoke for a few seconds, and then I told her to make her other calls and we would speak later. I also didn't want her to hear me cry.

In the end, Mackenzie, it's about the moment, not the moment before. And by the way, the bar exam is just a test. I'm proud of Jamie no matter what. But now she can bask in that achievement forever, whether or not she ever practices law.

And I will forever remember Jamie's moment before. I wonder if the homeless guy in Central Park still remembers mine.

All my everlasting love,

Dad

LUCKY AND LUCY HELPING YOU CELEBRATE CHRISTMAS

# Forty-Seven: Building a Furry Family

Dear Mackenzie,

Last week I had to go out of town. Since you and your mom have been living in NYC while you shoot *Nurse Jackie*, we had to board our dogs while I was away. As I went to pick them up this morning, I realized that though I sometimes complain about our overgrown pack of mutts, I was excited to see them.

Charlie was the last dog I ever bought. I use the past tense not because she's no longer with us. On the contrary, Charlie is alive and well and running amok in our house. I use the past tense because I will never buy another animal.

One day about seven years ago, you and your mom and I had lunch at a deli that was located near a pet store. Afterward, you asked if we could look at the "beautiful puppies." Against my better judgment we did, and predictably you fell in love with a cute little Pomeranian/Maltese mix. Then you did what most children tend to do when they want something. You pleaded with us to buy you this ball of fur.

I could tell that your mom loved the puppy too, but she stayed neutral, which emboldened me to put my foot down and say no. To my relief, we left the store puppyless.

That night at dinner, Jamie opined that Dixie could use a playmate (for more on Dixie, reread my letter to you called "Playing God"), but I held firm. Then the next day on my way home from work, I had the brilliant idea to surprise you with the puppy. Several hours and several thousand dollars later, Dixie had a playmate and Charlie had a home.

I told the story to a client of mine who is active in the world of pet rescue. She, in turn, told me about the horrors of puppy mills, and about the millions of wonderful shelter dogs each year whose owners can no longer keep them, or get tired of them and give them up, or abuse them and have them taken away, and then if the dogs don't get adopted within some period of time, they are euthanized. Once I educated myself on the issue, I vowed that if we ever wanted another pet, we would rescue one instead.

Not long after, your mom was out running errands and stopped to buy dog food. They were having a pet adoption day at the store, and she fell in love with a big, black mutt named Jackson. "That's the ugliest dog I've ever seen," I said when she showed us a picture. "And besides, the last thing we need is a third dog."

The next Saturday morning, the doorbell rang. "That must be Jackson," your mom said sheepishly. "I organized a play date for him with Dixie and Charlie. We don't have to keep him."

Now that's dirty pool, Mackenzie, but welcome to married life. You yelled, "Let's keep him!" before we even laid eyes on him. The woman from the adoption organization suggested we come meet him outside because "he's a little skittish." That turned out to be quite the understatement.

Jackson was huge. The moment he saw me, he started to growl ferociously, and the woman told me to "walk beside him and don't make eye contact." Seriously?

The first few weeks were tough. Jackson clearly had issues from his past and wasn't comfortable around people, especially men. And by men I mean me. Every time I walked into a room, Jackson would jump up, growl, and run away.

You loved him instantly, my sweet daughter, except the time early on when you played a little too roughly with him and he snapped at you. You ran into the living room crying hysterically. When we asked you what was wrong, you told us between tears, "I don't like Jackson anymore. Let's return him."

This was my chance to be rid of him. But I think rescue dogs, even ones who have known only abuse, have an instinct for real love. As you were crying, Jackson came up to you, rolled over, and started to squeal in apology. It was as if he'd had a chance to think it through and made the distinction between the roughhousing of an eight-year-old girl and someone trying to hurt him.

So Jackson became part of our family. And wouldn't you know it, in no time I couldn't get enough of him either. In a home where he experienced love instead of abuse, Jackson transformed into the sweetest, happiest animal you've ever seen. His deep, menacing bark is the only reminder of what his life before us might have been like.

Our experience with Jackson taught me a lot about the benefits of rescuing animals, and of the importance of love. It has reminded me that everyone deserves love, and benefits from love, and that love can overcome even the toughest circumstances. And I don't mean just with dogs.

When Dixie died, the pack went back down to two. Then one day I stumbled upon a place called Bark n' Bitches a pet store that rescues dogs from high-kill animal shelters and finds them homes. The owner told me she had "rehomed" over a thousand animals who would otherwise have been euthanized.

So we went there "just to look." You fell in love with a little Lhasa Apso mutt you immediately named Lucy. Lucy was beyond grungy, with hair so long and so matted you couldn't even see her eyes. She had just been rescued from the shelter and hadn't yet been bathed, taken to the vet, or otherwise checked out. But you were adamant this was the dog you wanted.

The owner told us we could come back in a few days to take Lucy home. When we came back, Lucy was bathed, had a haircut, and had something else we hadn't noticed before: a penis! It turns out Lucy was a he.

And of course while we were there your mom fell in love with some kind of poodle/terrier mix, and suggested we take that one too. Since I have no real clout in our family when it comes to these types of things, Lucy became Lucky, the terrier mix became Lucy, and now we have a pack of four.

And today, as Charlie, Lucky, and Lucy danced on my lap while we drove home and Jackson licked my ear, I said a little prayer of thanks for our motley furry family.

Don't tell your mom I admitted that.

All my everlasting love,

Dad

# Forty-Eight: Newtown, Connecticut

Dear Mackenzie,

A few months ago I wrote you a letter called "Evil" about the senseless killings in Aurora, Colorado. Sadly, it encompasses many of the themes and emotions I felt again as I read about the shooting at a school in Newtown, Connecticut. By all means reread it if you are moved to do so.

But today, as I hug you for dear life and tell you how much I love you, I'm feeling a bit differently about our individual and collective responsibility to put a stop to these heinous acts. So buckle up, my sweet daughter. Your dad is about to go on a rant.

For the past twenty-four hours, I've been reading the many comments on Facebook and Twitter about yesterday's horrific violence, which resulted in the deaths of twenty-eight people, twenty of them kids your age and even younger. No doubt the comments are all genuine and well intentioned. I too feel grief, loss, fear, nausea, regret, sympathy, vertigo, sadness, and many other emotions.

But far worse than any of those, I feel a sense of resignation that this is the new normal in America. I also feel a sense of unbridled anger that we as a people are unwilling to do anything about it even though we can.

Yes, us. And yes, unwilling.

No doubt we need better mental health care in this country. We need better parenting. Better guidance on movies and video games. Better everything, really. Check every box, as my friend Kyle likes to say. I hope by the time you're an adult, we're doing all of that a lot better than we are today.

But the immediate problem is guns.

Guns. Guns. Guns. Access to friggin' guns.

How is it that deranged, stupid, evil, insane people are able to legally access entire arsenals with which to kill our children? The answer is unfortunate and simple. It's because we are unwilling to do what it takes to stop them.

A fascinating statistic is making the rounds in social media outlets today. Here it is: If you added up the number of handgun deaths this year in Japan, Great Britain, Switzerland, Canada, Israel, Sweden, and Germany, and then multiplied that total by seventy, that outrageously high total would still be smaller than the number of handgun deaths this year in the United States alone. Are you kidding me?

Here's why, and we have to look in the mirror to see it.

First of all, 40 percent of people who are eligible to vote in the United States simply don't. What is that, fifty million people? Sixty million? More? Imagine if fifty million people went to the polls tomorrow and threw out every politician who refused to vote for real gun control reform. Real gun control reform would happen overnight. Why don't people vote? They can't be bothered? They think their vote doesn't matter? They're too cool? I don't know.

I have little doubt that even the most ardent opponents of gun control are horrified by this latest slaughter of innocents. We're all horrified. What sane person isn't? But being horrified is not enough. Your very life is at stake, Mackenzie. I hate to say it, but people who don't vote are part of this problem, and I can't forgive them for it.

Second, the gun lobby in this country is enormously well funded and effective. Politicians on both sides of the aisle take their money and become beholden to them. It's hard to blame them. They know they will not be voted out of office on that basis. Even those of us who vote rarely take the time to know or care who is funding our politicians. We put other selfish interests first. We have different priorities that make us look the other way. And we don't really believe that gun violence can happen to us or to our kids.

You're more interested in how your congressperson feels about lowering your personal tax rate than about the safety of our children? *Rat-at-at-at-at! Rat-at-at-at-at!*

You're more concerned with criminalizing gay marriage than about the safety of our children? *Pow! Pow! Pow! Pow! Pow!*

You're more excited about showing the length of your sexual organ in the "fiscal cliff" economic debate than about ensuring the safety of our children? *Boom! Ping! Ping! Boom!*

You don't think it can happen to your own son or daughter? *Boom! Boom! Boom! Boom! Boom! Rat-at-at-at-at! Pow! Pow! Pow! Rat-at-at-at!*

I know you can't vote for another few years, my little one. But I hope the adults around you will speak with the powerful weapon of their votes, and I hope they'll do it now. I pray the grief and horror we feel across this nation today will stir us to real action. Otherwise more heartbreak and tragedy await us.

And then no amount of prayers and condolences on Facebook and Twitter, or tearful recitations of beautiful Scripture, should make us feel one bit less guilty about our role in these terrible deaths.

All my everlasting love,

Dad

# Forty-Nine: The Meaning of Life

Dear Mackenzie,

Recently your mom took you to the American Museum of Natural History in New York. You must have enjoyed it, because a few weeks later you suggested we all go again together, and we did.

As we walked through the museum, I watched the different exhibits arouse your curiosity as you absorbed the various phenomena of nature. At each exhibit you took copious notes in a little spiral notebook for your science class. How much do you weigh on Mars? Check. Are human beings distant relatives of the Dimetrodon? Check. A fourteen-hundred-year-old sequoia tree lived in California and stood more than 300 feet tall? Check.

Seeing your wide-eyed wonder as the universe unfolded in front of you warmed my heart, and it was all I could do to not hug you every five seconds. Well, actually I did try to hug you every five seconds, and after the second or third time, you looked at me sternly and said, "Dad, stop!"

Then we went to see *Journey to the Stars* in the museum's planetarium. A presentation hosted by the voice of Whoopi Goldberg took us on a visual tour through our galaxy and beyond. Apparently there are hundreds of billions of stars in the Milky Way, plus trillions more in neighboring galaxies. Each star potentially fuels planets like our own that can sustain life.

Whoopi's voice explained how we came to have intelligent life on our planet. She also explained that our communications technology is now so advanced that if another life form anywhere in the galaxy has similarly advanced technology, we could easily talk to them. Apparently we're constantly dialing.

Yet the galaxy remains eerily silent. Can it be that with hundreds of billions of suns per galaxy, multiplied by the ten thousand galaxies visible through our powerful telescopes, that we alone got the magical elixir for intelligent life? The odds of that being the case make winning the lottery seem like a walk in the park.

Of all things, in the midst of so much science, I started to wonder about the meaning of life. Why are we here? Why do we die? Where are we going? I've always been more spiritual than existential, and I've always believed in a higher power. Yet my inner conflict between these two philosophical viewpoints rages on. Neither truly satisfies me.

On the spiritual side, what science doesn't explain is what we're all doing here and why no one else seems to be within earshot. There must be some grand design to our time on Earth. Right?

Are we just passing through on our way to who knows where? And if so, why should death even make us sad? What the caterpillar calls the end of the world, the master calls a butterfly, as Richard Bach once wrote.

The existential side isn't completely on point either. Even without a grand design, the question still remains: What are we all doing here, and why does no one else seem to be within earshot? And if we have no higher purpose, then why bother to move the human race forward while we're here? The opposite seems infinitely easier.

It's enough to make your head spin, and I don't have any good answers. The noted author Peggy Noonan may have summed it up best when she wrote, "Our generation, faced as it grew with a choice between religious belief and existential despair, chose marijuana. Now we're in our Cabernet stage."

Science. Religion. Life. Death. Existentialism. Minds much smarter than mine spend lifetimes contemplating these issues. It's easy to overthink it.

Then the other day I was going through some family photos, and I came across a picture of you on a horse named Charlie. You may not remember by the time you read this letter, but Charlie lived on your grandpa's farm. He was a beautiful Tennessee Walking Horse and you rode him a few times when you were three or four years old. Your grandpa also had a horse at the time named Sterling, whom you didn't ride but whom you would feed carrots to when we visited.

A few years ago, we were heading to Michigan for your grandpa's birthday and you started getting excited about riding Charlie again. And then shortly before our trip, Charlie up and died. You were only six at the time, and your mom and I worried about how best to tell you. In the end, we simply said that Charlie had died and hoped for the best.

You got upset and started to cry, and I told you that while it was sad Charlie had died, he had lived a long and happy life on Grandpa's farm. You asked me how old Charlie was when he died, and I said he was almost thirty, which I explained was quite old for a horse.

You thought about that for a second, and then asked me if Sterling was still alive and how old he was. I told you Sterling was indeed alive and that he was about fifteen years old. You paused for a moment as your mind processed that information. Then you smiled through your tears and said, "Oh, good."

Looking back, I realize that in that exchange, you intuitively answered some of the questions I was grappling with at the planetarium. You understood at the tender age of six that we live life in the here and now, and that while death is sad, we move beyond it by savoring life and by celebrating the living.

Maybe the meaning of life is as simple as that. Anything else you'd like to teach me?

All my everlasting love,

Dad

THE RED CARPET ON YOUR BIG NIGHT

# Fifty:
# Seeing the World Through Your Eyes

Dear Mackenzie,

One of the many wonderful things about being your father is that I get to experience the world anew through your eyes.

As a child, I never went to Disneyland. The time I first visited the park, I was already in my mid-twenties. It was a lot of fun and pretty amazing, to be sure. In fact, some of the nuances of Walt Disney's magnificent creation are probably better appreciated as an adult.

Yet I missed the chance to take in the marvel of Disneyland through a child's innocent eyes. Then I started going there with you, and I saw Disneyland in a new and wondrous way.

I'm having a similar experience right now, though not at Disneyland.

The Screen Actors Guild Awards happen every year around the last week of January. This year's ceremony will take place at the Shrine Auditorium in Los Angeles just a few weeks from now, on January 27.

The Academy Awards. The Emmys. The Golden Globes. Rarified air if you work in the entertainment industry. What could be more fulfilling, or better for your career, than hearing your name called after the words "and the Oscar goes to"? I can't even imagine. And yet over the years, many actors who have won those particular statuettes have told me that by far, the most humbling award an actor can receive is a SAG Award.

The SAG Awards are significant to an actor because your fellow actors fill out the ballots. Artisans who practice the same craft you do are acknowledging the excellence of your performance in a given film or television series. It's the ultimate validation.

On the morning of December 12, 2012, the SAG Award nominees were announced by Taye Diggs, an actor on a television series called *Private Practice*, and Busy Phillips (what a great name) who is on a series called *Cougar Town*. There was nothing out of the ordinary about the presentation or about the way those two individuals announced the nominations. Yet they will be forever etched in my mind. Why?

Because when Busy and Taye announced the nominees for Outstanding Performance by an Ensemble Cast in a Comedy Series, this was one of the nominated casts, in alphabetical order:

*NURSE JACKIE* (Showtime) MACKENZIE ALADJEM / Fiona Peyton EVE BEST / Dr. Ellie O'Hara BOBBY CANNAVALE / Dr. Mike Cruz JAKE CANNAVALE / Charlie Cruz PETER FACINELLI / Dr. Fitch Cooper EDIE FALCO / Jackie Peyton DOMINIC FUMUSA / Kevin Peyton ARJUN GUPTA / Sam LENNY JACOBSON / Lenny RUBY JERINS / Grace Peyton PAUL SCHULZE / Eddie Walzer ANNA DEAVERE SMITH / Gloria Akalitus STEPHEN WALLEM / Thor Lundgren MERRITT WEVER / Zoey Barkow

At the ripe old age of eleven, you, my sweet daughter, were nominated for a SAG Award!

I've attended every conceivable awards ceremony in my career. Over time I've had many clients nominated for various awards, and a number of them have won. I've been thanked for my efforts on national television. I've ridden in the limos, hung out at the parties, and done more than my share of hobnobbing with the rich and famous.

Now I grant you, I was never the one nominated, but just the same it's heady stuff. Yet I'm not sure I ever truly savored the experiences like I could or should have. On the contrary, I was usually lost in the demands of the moment. Did I introduce this actor to that director? Did John Doe spend enough time on the red carpet? Did Jill Doe make it out of the green room on time? Mostly it was just another day at the office, and a stressful one at that.

Your being nominated has made me look at it all from a whole new perspective.

I envision that over the next few weeks you'll have the time of your life. You've been invited to glamorous gifting suites that will make Christmas look like a dress rehearsal.

You'll attend the *Entertainment Weekly* nominees party at the famous Chateau Marmont Hotel, where you'll hobnob with stars, with producers and directors, and with studio and network executives. Do eleven-year-olds hobnob?

A well-known designer will give you an expensive new dress to wear to the ceremony. A professional stylist will make sure your hair and makeup look perfect on the day of the event. Showtime will send a car service to drive you to the ceremony and the glamorous after-party. It's as close to living the fairy tale as a young girl of any age could ever dream of.

And I am the proudest papa. My heart is filled with an innocent wonder that I thought was no longer possible for this old lion. Let me share with you the two pieces of advice I've given every client who has ever found herself or himself in this situation.

First, remember that the honor is in the nomination, and it will be yours for the rest of your life. Winning is frosting on the cake. I believe this to be true with all my heart. So have my clients, unless they ended up winning. Then they told me my advice was silly. At least until the next time they were nominated.

And second, savor the moment. You may be nominated ten more times in your career or never again. Bask in the glow of the paparazzi flashbulbs as you arrive on the red carpet. Be amazed at the people who are sitting next to you, and at the incredible company you're keeping. Enjoy the pit in your stomach as your category is called. Be humble if you win and keep your head up if you don't. Either way, it's all over much too quickly.

I'll be rooting for you and *Nurse Jackie* to win, of course. More important, I'll be experiencing my first awards show through your eyes, and marveling at how fun they really are.

All my everlasting love,

Dad

# Fifty-One:
# Things That Go Bump in the Night

Dear Mackenzie,

One night a few weeks ago, my cell phone rang at 3 AM. I groggily looked at the screen and saw that it was you calling me. I knew you were home and having a sleepover with your friend Peyton. That's weird.

"Hi," I mumbled into the phone. "Daddy," you said in an urgent whisper. "Come downstairs quick. Someone is breaking into the house." I bolted out of bed and down the stairs. In my fog, my mind was not processing what you were doing downstairs at that hour, or where Peyton was, or for that matter what I could possibly do to combat an intruder if indeed there was one. In the nanosecond that it took me to get downstairs, I had a horrible flashback.

Many years ago, the year I graduated from law school, I spent the summer studying for the bar exam. My girlfriend at the time, Lisa Bernfeld, lived in a small two-bedroom apartment in a sketchy part of town. But the rent was cheap, and when you're young you feel immortal, so neither of us paid too much attention to our surroundings.

Throughout that summer, I would often study late into the night with my good friend and classmate Jon Panzer and then head over to Lisa's apartment. I would bring all my notes and study books with me to her place and then go to the review class in the morning.

Lisa had a roommate, and her roommate also had a boyfriend. Since neither she nor her roommate knew who would be sleeping over when, they each got in the habit of closing their respective bedroom doors at night. On this particular night, Lisa knew her roommate wouldn't be coming home but we closed the bedroom door anyway. Force of habit.

At about 2:30 AM, Lisa shook me awake and whispered, "Someone's broken into the apartment." As I started to tell her she was imagining it, I saw a light go on inside the apartment and heard several sets of footsteps. My heart jumped to my throat and Lisa whispered, "What should we do?"

All of us hope, my sweet daughter, that we will act courageously if and when that need ever arises. But I can tell you from experience that no amount of planning can prepare you for a moment like that. As I write you this letter almost thirty years later, I am still embarrassed by the first thought that went through my mind. It was: "Please, God, don't let them steal my bar review materials, or I will fail the exam." I hope Lisa can forgive me.

I put the absurdity of that thought out of my head and tried to think. Whoever was in there was making a lot of noise, and we were both petrified with fear. In a whisper of my own, I asked if it was possible her roommate had come home, but Lisa responded that her roommate was out of town. Besides, we could hear whoever was out there dismantling the stereo system, which I seriously doubted her roommate would be doing at 2:30 AM.

"Go out there and see what's going on," Lisa whispered to me. Now I loved my girlfriend, but there was no way I was going out there. Whoever had broken in was not being at all quiet, and was taking their sweet time robbing the place. To me that meant that either the burglars thought no one was home, in which case surprising them didn't seem like a good idea, or they didn't care if anyone was home, which seemed even worse.

I called 911. Now, this was in the days before cell phones, and to make matters worse, my girlfriend's apartment still had one of those old rotary phones, not a push-button one. So when I dialed the phone, it sounded like machine gun fire. The 911 operator put me on hold. Then she hung up on me, hopefully by mistake. I kid you not.

I didn't dare try to dial again. So we lay in bed, no doubt silently praying, for about twenty minutes, which in that situation seemed like an interminably long time. At one point we heard the footsteps coming toward us, and we could see shadows by our bedroom door.

They lingered there for a few seconds and then retreated. Lisa later told me that at that moment, she was going to whisper to me that she loved me, but she had this vision that if she said that, the door would burst open and we would be killed. So she stayed silent.

At some point the sounds stopped. We lay there for at least fifteen more minutes, and then I softly opened the bedroom door. The burglars were gone, and so was the sound system and everything else that wasn't nailed down. Well, except for my bar exam study notes. For some inexplicable reason, those didn't interest the thieves. You'd think they would at least have taken my notes on criminal law. We called the police, who came and took a report, and then we went to Junior's Deli to celebrate that we were still alive.

All of that raced through my head as I bolted downstairs. You and Peyton were huddled in the media room, where you had fallen asleep hours earlier watching a movie. "The bell on the alarm system chimed," you said. "There's a lady with her hands on her hips in your backyard," added Peyton.

Adrenaline pumping, I quickly scanned the downstairs and fortunately no one was there. The "lady with her hands on her hips" turned out to be a chair by the pool. And I showed you and Peyton that the alarm had been triggered by a set of French doors, still locked, that sometimes got toggled by the wind. I hugged you both, and I told you that nothing bad will ever happen to you as long as your mom or I, or your older sisters, are with you. You gave me a kiss, and the two of you went upstairs to bed. Before doing the same, I said a little prayer of thanks.

In truth, the notion that nothing bad can happen to you if you are with us is more a meditation than a certainty. But I'll keep saying it to you, and I hope you keep believing it, and I would not hesitate to do whatever it took to will that prayer into reality.

Of course, a little luck and some divine providence wouldn't hurt either.

All my everlasting love,

Dad

OF THEE I SING

# Fifty-Two: Fifty-Two Weeks

Dear Mackenzie,

Fifty-two weeks. Twelve months. One year.

A small fraction of the average human life span. The blink of an eye in the history of time.

About a year ago, I decided to try to write you a letter each week for a year. And now, fifty-two letters later, I am done.

In many ways, I suspect these letters reveal more about me than about you or your sisters. I spent part of the last year in physical therapy rehabilitating a broken ankle. My physical therapist, a talented young woman named Sharon Lagman-Mino, would laugh at me every week. "You address the letters to Mackenzie," she would say, "and then you write about you."

Sharon was probably right, but that's okay. Maybe subconsciously that was no accident. How you and I will experience each other when you're an adult and I'm an old man is different than how we experience each other now, when you're still very young and I'm still reasonably vibrant. I wanted to capture that snapshot for both of us. I hope I did.

So these letters are about you and the world as I experienced you and it over the course of one year. No more and no less.

Fifty-two weeks of my thoughts about life, love, family, faith, and how to negotiate a bigger allowance.

Fifty-two weeks of meditations about your place in my heart, and hopefully about my place in yours.

Fifty-two weeks of lessons for the both of us to learn.

May these letters guide you and comfort you.

May they give you a boost and a helping hand as you go through life.

May they bring abundant joy and a few smiles to you and your sisters, and to your future families.

May they forever remind you how much your mom and I love all three of you with every breath we take.

Many years ago, when I was just a boy, I was sitting around with your great-grandma Granny Goldberg and your great-grandma Lilly. "May you live to one hundred and twenty," Granny Goldberg said at one point. Your great-grandma Lilly smiled and replied, "and why would you limit him to only one hundred and twenty?" She was only half kidding.

By the time you're the age I am as I write to you now, most likely your mom and I won't be physically around. But if we are, my sweet daughter, we'll remind you to be bold and courageous. We'll remind you to dare and to risk. We'll remind you to love fully and profoundly. We'll remind you to be kind and considerate. And, most important, we'll remind you to see life for the amazing adventure that it is.

When I set out to write you these letters, I never imagined the personal fulfillment and satisfaction that I would get from writing them. And in the end, the joy that you, Heather, Jamie, and your wonderful mom give me each and every day is more than should even be legal.

Now and forever, of thee I sing.

All my everlasting love,

Dad

# Acknowledgments

This book was an act of love, and many people helped bring it to life. My heartfelt thanks go to so many of our friends, too numerous to name here, who read blog entries and encouraged me to keep writing. Thank you to Peter McGuigan, Claire Harris, and the team at Foundry Literary + Media, who didn't laugh at me when I asked if they thought this could be a book, and who are amazing at what they do. Thank you to Anthony Ziccardi, Dan Vidra, and Michael Wilson at Post Hill Press for taking a chance and publishing a book by someone completely unknown. Huge thanks to Michael Shohl, who edited the manuscript with an artist's touch, and who made both the book and me better. Thank you to our daughters Heather Hughes and Jamie Hughes, who have graced me with unconditional love and acceptance from the moment I came into their young lives. And thank you to the inimitable Mackenzie Aladjem, who not only inspired these stories, but whose indomitable spirit and fierce independence keep me on my toes. Finally, and with all the love in my heart, thank you to my wife, Laura, the soul mate, partner in love and life, and best friend, to whom I said a sheepish hello one fateful night at a skating rink in East Cleveland all those years ago.

# About the Author

Norman Aladjem was born in Montevideo, Uruguay, and has truly lived the American dream. After graduating from UCLA Law School, he started his career as an entertainment attorney, then became a talent agent. He is currently the CEO of Mainstay Entertainment, a talent management and film/TV production company. He lives in Los Angeles with his family and their four dogs.